By the same author

PLACES IN THE SUN
FOREIGN AFFAIRS
FREEDOM AND ORDER
DAYS FOR DECISION

The Eden Memoirs:
FULL CIRCLE
FACING THE DICTATORS
THE RECKONING
TOWARDS PEACE IN INDO-CHINA

Another World
1897—1917

Anthony Eden
Earl of Avon K.G., P.C., M.C.

ALLEN LANE

Contents

List of Plates

Author's Note

I wish to apologize in advance to any old friends who still have memories of Windlestone days as we knew them, for any mistakes of fact I may have made.

The two drawings from *Notes Prises au Front* by my friend André Dunoyer de Segonzac are reproduced by kind permission of Madame de Segonzac. The letters of George Moore which appear in the text are quoted by kind permission of Mr J. C. Medley and Mr R. G. Medley, owners of the copyright in George Moore; and the letters of Walter Sickert are quoted by kind permission of Mr Henry Lessore. I am grateful to Sir John Eden for permission to reproduce the painting of Sir William Eden by Prince Pierre Troubetskoy, and the painting of Lady Eden by Sir Hubert von Herkomer. The water-colour of Windlestone, east front, by Sir William Eden is reproduced by kind permission of Lord Brooke.

I would also like to express my thanks to the Public Record Office in London, and to the Rifle Depot at Winchester, for giving me access to the battalion's War Diaries, and to a number of fellow riflemen in the Yeoman Rifles, particularly to the late Mr Robert Iley M.M., for permission to quote from his diary, to Mr Gerald Dennis for his remarkable memory and personal records of the battalion's history, and to Mr Norman Carmichael M.M. for his friendship and counsel.

Above all, I want to thank my wife whose patient encouragement and care made this small book possible.

A proportion of any royalties received for this book will be donated to the Rifleman's Aid Society and to the Royal Air Force Benevolent Fund (Simon Eden Memorial).

I

Brabazon and Barbizon

A few years ago, in my old age, I had occasion to pass along the Great North Road, south of Rushyford in County Durham. Here the gentle rolling farmland seemed still to take on that special and satisfying pattern which shows some hand has been at work planting and composing the land-scape. In my mind's eye I could remember every vista, every tree.

I turned in from the south up the drive to Windlestone. There it was, apparently intact; the roof whole, the windows glazed. Yet what had been spacious and elegant was now gaunt and vacantly lonely. The curved and squat outlines of some Nissen huts crowded up against the north front windows and the lake had lost its limpidity under a green mask.

My eyes travelled sadly along the avenue that led to the chapel. Here was frank ruin. The building lay open to the sky with the family memorial plaques removed from the walls and taken to my brother's new home in the heaths of Hampshire. The avenue of yews down which I had so often walked was still intact; only as I peered I realized they were not yews at all but ilex trees.

So do the customs and legends of one's youth become fixed in memory, inaccurate and distorted maybe, but the only link one has with another world.

*

'Come with me little boy and I will teach you the difference between Brabazon and the Barbizon School.' This was my introduction to what was then called modern painting, a title which Mr George Moore had recently chosen for a book of essays which he had dedicated to my father. 'Modern painting,' wrote Mr Moore, 'has been the subject of nearly all our conversations in the past, and I suppose will be the subject of many conversations in the future.'

For me, not yet in my teens, the lesson was something of an ordeal. It was not so much the Corot with its road stretching through an easy, softly wooded landscape, that presented difficulty. Even Mr Brabazon's water-colours made a pleasing if somewhat confused impression, with their unexpected streaks of white. It was the larger, earlier pictures on either side of the mantlepiece, lacking detailed drawing and coloured vivid as rainbows, which utterly perplexed me. 'Can you see what that is?' asked my father. I shook my head and he looked disappointed. 'It is a ship going down in a storm.' I had not proved worthy of my first viewing of a Turner water-colour.

The enormous problems of childhood linger in the memory. I was puzzled why Windlestone, my home, which evidently had already ample supplies of paintings for its rooms and corridors, appeared always to be receiving more. To my mind a picture was something to fill a gap on the wall; when there were no gaps, why did new pictures keep arriving?

As time passed, this problem came to matter less and I began to make my own selection which I would visit at the beginning of my holidays and say good-bye to at the close, though still ranking definitely after my pony or 'David', the small Aberdeen terrier which had been entrusted to my younger brother and myself before school days began.

The pictures at Windlestone fell naturally into three categories. Those paintings bought by my grandfather, chiefly in Spain, a country he knew well and where he loved to travel. Next came the family portraits, relatively few in number but above average in quality. Finally there were the modern paintings which my father was occasionally buying and discussing endlessly with his friends.

I had three favourites in those early years. An angel by Alonso Cano was a typical sculptor's painting and its impressive realism, if an angel can be real, was probably its appeal. My other preferred paintings conformed more to childish tastes. An enchanting little Murillo of Tobias and his fish was gentle in colour and sentimental in treatment. No doubt it was sentiment also which kept me entranced before a Lawrence of a child painted after death. The child, a member of the family, was very pretty and the darkened wing of an angel swept down behind his head.

I could feel no comparable interest in the portrait of Barbara Villiers. She seemed a cold, almost forbidding character, nor did the information that she was an ancestress carry much conviction. Not at least until many years later when, in the course of an official visit to Sweden as an Under-Secretary at the Foreign Office, I was presented with an elaborate genealogical table tracing my descent to a saintly early Swedish king. The connecting link, incongruously enough, was Barbara.

Maynard Keynes, who was somewhat unexpectedly interested in such by-ways of history, asked me one day when we were both with Winston Churchill enjoying the rare gastronomic treat of a luncheon with the Spanish Ambassador in war-time London, whether it was true that I had Villiers blood. I said that it seemed so and told him the Swedish story. He took it seriously and was soon rattling off the names of Villiers' descendants of whom he thought highly, including the Duke of Alba's cousin and principal guest at that luncheon.

As I grew older, the pictures my father was buying began to intrigue me more. I made progress the easy way, through the Fantin Latours, especially one of white roses. There were six of his flower pieces by the time my father died.

William Eden had a comfortable income, but he liked to spend it. My mother used to tell me that every penny he received from rents went back into the estate. I can believe this, but it did not all go in improvements to farm buildings or cottages, though these were well cared for, with every door and window repainted a deep shade of blue every two or three years. Much was spent in embellishing the estate, with trees being planted more for effect than profit. Nothing was stinted anywhere within or without the house, so that if there were no shortages, there were also no savings.

As the estate was entailed, this was no great matter and my father was probably right, certainly in the context of the years before 1914, in his oft-repeated conviction that his heir, my brother Jack, would be a richer man than he. There remained the question of the younger children. My sister Marjoric, the eldest of the family, had received a settlement on her marriage, but she still ranked in law as a younger child, as did three out of four of my father's sons, Timothy, myself and Nicholas. For these the settlement was insignificant compared with that of my father's two younger brothers, who had each received, so my mother often insisted, £50,000 and an estate in Yorkshire.

When pressed on these matters, my father would reply: 'But I am buying pictures for them.' Though it is true that he left the pictures, furniture and silver he had bought to be sold for his younger children, that answer carried no conviction at the time with trustees or friends who knew of his intention, while it caused dissension and hard feelings later. The immediate criticism was chiefly because the paintings my father was buying were incomprehensible or worse to his contemporaries.

Among our nearest neighbours was the Londonderry family whose Durham estates and coal mines lay a few miles east and north-east of Windlestone. It was the Lord Londonderry of my childhood who once muttered to a fellow guest: 'You know, something ought to be done about it. Willie actually gave good money for these things.' Quite likely it was the Degas *Washerwomen* which provoked this comment, for I have a water-colour by my father of this painting as it hung over his writing-table between a Corot and a Mark Fisher. 'My own immaculate Degas,' he called it. I remember it well hanging there.

It would not be fair to mock our north-country neighbours. We all date somewhere. I am conscious that I do myself. Most abstract art is a closed book to me and, while I consider Picasso one of the greatest draughtsmen of all time, and his Blue Period among the world's finest painting, I cannot feel quite the same towards some of his later work, particularly the colour. It is on this account that of the two cubist founders, I generally prefer Braque of the twenties and thirties.

After the First World War when I went up to Oxford I joined in forming a small club, the Uffizi, such as used to mushroom at Oxford in those days, and I hope does still. Our purpose was to discuss the arts, ancient and modern, and I have described elsewhere* my unsuccessful embassage to Ebury Street to my father's old friend, George Moore, to ask him to read a paper to us on Cézanne. He made no attempt to conceal his principal objection, which was that he did not really like Cézanne's paintings. Why should he? His loves were the works of Manet, Monet, Degas and Berthe Morisot, and there or thereabouts he stopped.

If I had had a little more experience and admiring as I did Moore's own collection, I would have asked him to speak of one of his favourites. He would possibly have accepted, despite his complaint that it would have taken him three weeks to prepare his paper, and we at Oxford would have enjoyed an illuminating evening.

As it was, he told me of an incident with my father. One day when the two men were to have luncheon together in Paris my father was late and when he did arrive wanted at once to tell George Moore the reason. It seems that he had just been to an exhibition of the works of a painter who was new to him. He had been deeply impressed by these pictures and had asked the gallery to reserve a number of them. George Moore poured cold water on all this. If my father wanted another picture, why did he not buy another painting by Degas? He knew where he was with him, and surely he could not possess too many works by an artist he admired so deeply. Moore apparently over-persuaded my father. At any rate he did not buy the pictures; the painter was Cézanne.

I thought it candid of Mr Moore to tell me that story though it saddened me as I had recently seen an exhibition of Cézanne in Venice, including such lovely things as *Le Garçon au Gilet Rouge*. The tale did not shock then as it would now.

* *Full Circle*, Cassell, 1960.

We were still at the period when Clive Bell could write in indignant protest that the Tate Gallery had refused the gift of six Cézannes while finding room for some new works by Professor Tonks.

*

I was very fond of Windlestone. As I knew it would never be mine, my affection was not possessive. I loved its spaciousness and the knowledge that within it I could find beauty, reading and entertainment for any mood. The house, built by Bonomi about 1840, was a classic rectangle of sandstone, with a strong colonnade protecting the downstairs rooms on the east front, and a surprisingly delicate balustrade with spaced urns at roof level. In the north of England the houses of the landowners were large and their estates also. My father had therefore inherited a handsome property but no more, perhaps less, remarkable than those of our neighbours.

By the time I was conscious of my surroundings he had made it into something 'rich and rare'. Alas that the transformation of a house or a garden or a park should be so vulnerable to time, because more even than in his water-colour painting, my father had created Windlestone, as only an artist could, as a personal harmony. The Impressionists kept company with the Old Masters, the graceful Hepple-white dining room chairs might have been bought, but others had been rescued from a loft over the stable buildings to which they had been relegated in Victorian days, and the splendid William and Mary leather screen had been discovered above some cupboards in the old laundry.

The formal Victorian garden was submerged in schemes of colour, with the pervading scent of lavender and rosemary and sweet briar. My father built the terraces which set off Bonomi's architecture and, above all, thinned and planted at every angle from the house until the trees were Windlestone's chief glory. It was the same within the house. Apart from pictures and furniture, the decoration, the curtains, the library kept up to date, all these taught, beguiled, even inspired any visitor in the least sensitive to beauty.

In the summer of 1914, my father had covered the walls of his sitting-room with a faded indigo paper found in a shop in

Bishop Auckland. He was proud of this as a background for his pictures. In the East Hall, which ran nearly the full length of the house and was lit from domes above as well as from the east windows, he had overpainted the dull red flock paper in black. The effect was strangely glowing, and the earlier Baltimore portraits, the two best very fine examples of Mytens and Soest, looked splendid against it in their finely carved Jacobean frames. A primitive by Juan Juanes and a sweeping Paul Veronese seemed at home there too; and over the mantelpiece, perhaps the finest of the Spanish pictures, a portrait by Francesco de Ribalta of the painter and his wife.

Into the adjoining West Hall, my father had introduced some Charles II panelling from the Manor House at West Auckland. There were our arms with those of our north-country neighbours with whom we had inter-married, some-times more than once. Lambton, Bee and Hutton, the lamb, the bee and the eagle; they were all there together with one, which, if rightly identified, was from farther afield, that of the Black Cumming. I hoped that the report was true because I admired him.

To the south of the West Hall was the dining room which my father had repainted in another blue, the colour of a madonna's robes in an Italian picture. This was a large room in which he had hung some eighteenth- and early nineteenth-century family portraits and some more recent ones, including Sargent's portrait of my mother. I never liked that painting, for all its brilliance, and I don't think my father did either. My mother was sitting playing patience with her head twisted at an unnatural angle, which caused *Punch* to dub it *The Spiral Staircase*. I preferred Sargent's more conventional drawing, but more to my taste than either was Wilson Steer's portrait of her, which Mr Steer's trustees later kindly gave to me, having found it unframed in his studio at his death. My mother was then alive and I asked her how it came about that the picture was still in Steer's possession, as it appeared to have been painted about 1890. Her memory was that the artist had not been entirely satisfied with it, and had taken it away to work on.

The most dated of the many portraits of my mother was a Herkomer painted in her early twenties soon after her marriage, in evening dress, out-of-doors against a Windlestone landscape. Absurd, but the head is a very lovely likeness. My mother told me that Sir Hubert von Herkomer painted this mainly from photographs, of which he took a large number. More sympathetically of the period was a portrait by Jacques-Emile Blanche; but most enchanting of all was a drawing of her asleep in the garden by Sickert. I have no idea who has it now.

In the library, my favourite room in the house, my father had made few changes. It had remained virtually unaltered since the house was rebuilt by Sir Robert Johnson Eden early in the nineteenth century. Building and books were his obsession. An only son, and his mother being an heiress, he could afford to indulge himself. The library was his principal achievement. On three sides of the room from floor to ceiling the walls were books, cut across three-quarters of the way up by a gallery with brass balustrading. The shelves had been let into the walls and divided by delicate mahogany pilasters. The only breaks in the vista of bindings were the mahogany door into the room from the East Hall, and a very fine eighteenth-century mantelpiece, presumably a survivor from the old house, in the west wall.

In a corner were several rows of skilfully designed dummy books, one above the other. In one of these rows a catch was concealed which the initiated could press to open a door upon a small staircase which led to the gallery, giving easy access to the higher shelves. It can be imagined what joy a secret knowledge of that catch was in boyhood games of hide-and-seek.

Sir Robert was said to haunt a corner of the gallery and to be seen occasionally, an old man poring over a book. So at least my sister and an Auckland cousin, himself a book lover, used to assure me. I can only report that I spent many hours alone there and never saw Sir Robert or anyone else to disturb the atmosphere of the most soothing room in the house.

My mother told me that my grandfather, who was a

frugal man and a classical scholar, would lie there by the hour of an evening reading by the light of a tallow candle and wrapped in a rug, to save the cost of a fire. This hardly seemed to me a likely story either, in a house where coal was free.

My father refused to treat his library only as a period piece. Every year Mr Humphreys of Hatchards would arrive from London, go through the books and advise on new editions. The overflow was kept in eighteenth-century book-cases in the West Hall and in my father's own room.

II

Retreat to the Continent

121 Ebury Street.
10 February

My dear Friend or my dear Sybil – whichever address pleases
you, let me tell you that your letter was a pleasure to receive and
in a way compensated me for my disappointment. The parlourmaid had just walked out of the house without telling anybody
she was going and after borrowing a couple of pounds from me.
The cook was very angry and to escape from her I dined at a
restaurant in Sloane Square close by. I might have taken you
there or elsewhere if I had thought of it but one doesn't think
adequately in these constantly occurring domestic crises. But you
will be in London again. . . So you are leaving Windlestone, but
not for good. My house on the hill-top in Ireland will become a
ruin and many houses in England will too; another fifty years
will see the end of life as we knew it. But where are you going to
live when you leave Windlestone? You don't say and that is just
what I'd like to know. In London I hope. The lease of this house
is up in three years and then – it is useless to look ahead but I look
forward to seeing you.

Always affectionately yours,
George Moore

The family was leaving Windlestone because, when I was
about three years old, the agent absconded to the United
States with all the cash he could lay hands on, leaving a heap
of unpaid bills. It was skilfully done and took the accountants
quite a while to discover. My father dealt with this setback
by sending his entire family, together with courier, maids,
nannies and governess, on a peregrination of Europe while
he tried to sort out the tangle.

Our first stop was Nice, where we took a large white villa called Beausite, now, I believe, a nursing home, on the outskirts of the town. The light seemed bright to bewilderment; there is a snapshot of me standing in front of the house, my shorts too loose for me, with my eyes puckered up in the sunshine. The house and garden were on the slope of a hill and presumably commanded a view to the Mediterranean. From my height I was only aware of things in my immediate vision. I was much astonished by the curious shape of the palm trees and the many strange fruits, tangerines, oranges and 'nèfle de japon'. This last, with its unique aromatic tang, a cross between medlar and mango, became my favourite, perhaps so persuaded by our French governess.

In the garden there also grazed at times my brother Timothy's tame sheep, to which he was much attached but which preferred to knock me down. There were other risks too. One afternoon we were lifting stones and discovered an unpleasant-looking animal about an inch long with a tail. My brother encouraged me to pick it up, but some instinct made me doubtful. At this juncture a grown-up came to see what we were at, chided us and dealt with the scorpion.

While we were marking time at Beausite the annual battle of flowers at Nice came round. This ended badly for my mother, who was driving in one of the open carriages. My brother and I were watching from the roadside and throwing flowers ourselves. We saw her go waving by, but it was not until we arrived home and found her in a darkened room that we learnt that the stalk from a bunch of flowers had hit her in the eye.

It must have been soon after this accident that our French maid came bouncing into her mistress's room one morning announcing with glee, '*La reine est morte, la reine est morte!*' My mother rebuked her grimly, but we were less successful when French boys would yell after us in the streets of Nice, '*Vivent les Boers!*'

We spent other and shorter spells in France, at Paris-Plage, then a small village of ugly Victorian villas. A safe beach stretched to the horizon, which did not prevent a bather drowning one day, but to my chagrin I was not allowed near the casualty. At Paris-Plage lessons were dominant, under the eye of a stern but capable French governess, my shortcomings resulting in many spells in the corner. My mother was sometimes absent in Paris, and Mademoiselle Drouin then had charge of us. We used to go by coastal train from Étaples, Paris-Plage and Le Touquet, through Neuchâtel and other local stations to Boulogne, for German lessons given by two charming old ladies, the Mesdemoiselles Koch, in a house near the ramparts. Sometimes as a reward I would visit a wonderful pastry shop called Cavinques, with its bowl of whipped cream, spooned skilfully between two halves of meringue before my delighted eyes.

Much of our enjoyment in France was due to a French family who were our close friends, the de Bellets. The Baron was impeccably dressed and a gay and skilful conversationalist who admired my mother, could talk gardening with my father and was always kindly to the Eden children. His family seemed better brought up, better mannered and much better educated than we were. They knew what to say in French and English and how to handle themselves. François could shoot well, and I little guessed during our childish games that Pauline was a future golf champion of France. François, who was between my two elder brothers in age, was a good-looking boy constantly praised by my mother for all the virtues, without doing him any harm in our eyes. His death in the First World War seemed especially sad.

The Jean de Bellets often came to stay at Windlestone, winter and summer. A temporary coldness intervened during the Dreyfus case. I remember being with my father and Johnnie de Bellet in the chapel walk at home, when suddenly a terrible row blew up over some incident in that long drama. I had only the vaguest idea of what it was all about. Sixty years later, staying at St Paul de Vence, I was drinking a particularly delicious *vin rosé*. It came from the de Bellet vineyards.

Our sojourn abroad ended in Dresden, where we took a villa with a garden. Here my father joined us and here George Moore wrote to him:

If I can get to Dresden in August it will be nice. I have written five Essays* and the book will contain a dozen so you see I shall have nearly finished the book by August. The book is only my conversation put into shape, but some people and I think you are among the number think that that is the best part of me.

I wonder you don't come to paint in Ireland, the country is so beautiful.

Yes, my dear friend, we are getting old but our friendship is a pleasant memory and I think we shall always be friends. You are 'an awfully good fellow', one of the best hearted and I am proud to be your friend. I am glad you have paid off your debts; it was a terrible struggle no doubt – a load of debt like that is not easily got rid of. You see an Agent is peace and happiness or else anxiety and ruin. Every landlord seems to fall in with one bad Agent, if he falls in with a second he is certainly ruined.

Goodbye for the present.
Yours as ever
George Moore

No doubt it was due to my mother's wise selection that I was happy in nursery days under the firm but patient care of Nannie Ward. Even during our travels abroad I do not remember more than occasional ructions between Nannie and the sequence of French and German governesses.

We were taught by Mademoiselle Drouin, who accompanied us during all our European peregrinations. I enjoyed her lessons, not least because she had made me presents of splendidly illustrated French books, one of French history and the other of the Bible. I revelled in the drawings and was only too happy to read and discuss the small print which accompanied them. Mademoiselle Drouin was certainly a highly intelligent woman, and a good teacher who deserved a more receptive class than Nicholas and myself. Though I liked to work with her and she persevered with me, the younger Nicholas did not enjoy her lessons or her strict discipline, and one day as we were climbing the stairs I heard him muttering behind us: 'Old drain, old drain.' Mademoiselle Drouin was soon to have a more attentive pupil.

* *Modern Painting.*

Mrs Patrick Campbell was a frequent visitor to Windlestone, sometimes with her daughter Stella, more nearly my sister Marjorie's contemporary, who was I thought very beautiful and whom I saw as an ideal Roxane in a production of *Cyrano* after the war. Mrs Pat herself we all enjoyed. Vitality, charm, together with a sweeping no-nonsense air which usually resulted in a shattering and calculated indiscretion, always assured her an eager welcome and a rapt audience.

Despite so much public and private acclaim, Mrs Pat could always find time to be thoughtful and generous to the young. Years later, when I was a subaltern in war-time Aldershot, an unexpected leave gave two or three of us an opportunity for a London theatre. We decided upon *Pygmalion*, but at such short notice no tickets were to be had. With temerity I approached Mrs Pat and the outcome was a stage box and a wonderful evening. When the curtain fell I went back-stage to say 'thank you'. We spoke of my father who had died within the year. Mrs Pat concluded: 'I am glad that your father cannot see me now. If he could, do you know what he would say?' 'He would praise you for so marvellous a performance,' I replied eagerly. Mrs Pat smiled and shook her head: 'No,' she said sadly, 'he would say "Woman how coar-r-se you have become." '

That evening was many years ahead. Meanwhile the problem was very different. Mrs Pat had undertaken to act with Sarah Bernhardt in *Pélleas et Mélisande*, a formidable task in any circumstances but made more so in this instance because Mrs Pat's French was not impeccable. The answer was Mademoiselle Drouin, and a triumphant success it proved, though I was never allowed to see the play and could only make the most of unexpected holidays from French lessons.

On her visits Mrs Pat was invariably accompanied by a Pekingese, usually of advanced age and often, we thought, of doubtful allurements. Any criticism we might feel had to be sternly repressed for Pekes ruled supreme in her affections, to the point where her name appeared in the Windlestone visitors' book: 'Stella Patrick Campbell and Pinkie Ponkie Pooh'.

*

Once re-established at Windlestone, a new reign opened with the arrival of an English governess. Miss Broomhead, soon rechristened 'Doodles' as being Nicholas's poor effort to recall her name, was small, quiet and blonde, but we soon learnt that she could be firm not only with us but on our behalf. Our day nursery was transformed into a schoolroom and my rocking-horse, to which I was much attached, banished to a distant corner. I was provided with a desk and all concerned instructed that lesson hours were not to be interrupted.

My brother Timothy, four years my senior and now a schoolboy, had been apt during his holidays to drift into the nursery at will. One day he came in as usual, interrupted our lessons and began to twit and tease me. Doodles watched for a while and then got up from her chair, walked up to Timothy, took him by the shoulder and propelled him firmly through the door he had left open, saying, 'Don't you dare come in here again during lesson hours.' I watched awe-struck and could only exclaim, 'There will be trouble over this,' fearing my brother's appeal to my mother. 'I don't think so,' replied Doodles quietly, and she was right. Doodles remained at Windlestone for thirty years, with an interlude as quartermaster when the house became a hospital in the First World War. She ended by teaching Timothy's own children.

Soon after Miss Broomhead's rule was established, I was given much more latitude and allowed to visit the many craftsmen working on the estate at Windlestone. The carpentering and paint shops had long been popular and I had served a brief and enjoyable, but on my part clumsy, apprenticeship with the Burlinson family at the former. They were masters of their art; their daily fare might be gates or window frames for a farmhouse, or to rehang pictures for my father, but they were no less capable of making an elegant copy of a Sheraton sideboard, just as their predecessors had done a century earlier.

Not so far away was a new and rival attraction, the electric light engine which had been recently installed. This was presided over by young Jackson, who was expert and likeable.

He would proudly show us his engine all polished up and beautiful, though his craft was a complete mystery to me then and still is. Other acceptable excursions were to the stables to feed our ponies and inspect the hunters of the grown-ups and the carriage horses, particularly 'Manners' and 'Yankee', under the Irish stud-groom Shoebottom's guidance, or to the game larder with the head game-keeper, Peter Smitton, to see the outcome of a recent shoot. Equal in appeal to any of these was a visit to Hall the blacksmith, a solid and friendly man; I could have stayed indefinitely by the bright glow of his forge.

Less certain in their attraction were the greenhouses. I liked the vineries, especially the muscats, dozens of bunches of grapes hanging there, all with the lovely bloom on them, but they did make me feel greedy and of course I must not touch them. And then there was always the risk of running into my father, perhaps in the new carnation house which he had just built. My reception would then be uncertain; at best I might be greeted and have an overblown bloom picked for me, at worst I was definitely surplus to the work in hand.

At Windlestone there were no huge period set pieces of flowers nor a plethora of potted palms, despite the many greenhouses. I do not think that my father much cared to have flowers indoors, though they would occasionally appear on the dining room table and my mother's boudoir was suitably embowered. On shooting parties and other festive occasions there would be a buttonhole for every man, a gardenia or perhaps a carnation.

Our nurseries lay at the northern end of the front of the house with a spacious view to rolling blue hills on the horizon. These hills fascinated me and I told Doodles one day that I wanted to make an expedition to walk to them. Doodles demurred that they were very far. However, when I persisted, she wisely allowed me to learn for myself. A day or two later we set out, I having decided that we should progress across the fields. We had walked for perhaps two miles when I had to admit that the hills were still no nearer and dejectedly I retraced my steps. My objective had been the Hambleton hills, at least twenty miles from Windlestone.

Sometimes in the morning, usually after breakfast, but occasionally while we were still dressing, my father would come along the corridor to visit his youngest sons in the nursery. After kissing us both, he would stand for a moment or two in friendly rather than formidable catechism. Nicholas and I enjoyed these visits, not only because my father could charm us but because we were less likely to be corrected as could so easily happen when on our ponies or in the garden.

Outside the nursery there were two diversions. On the north side were the stone stairs, curving up from the passage below which led to the billiard room. At the top of the stairs, well lit from a dome above, was a large Guercino of Joseph receiving the attentions of Potiphar's wife. I could not make out what the picture was about and I found Doodle's explanation unsatisfying. Then in the passage by the night nursery door hung a tribute to the current craze for gymnastics, some parallel bars fixed there by the Burlinsons. On these Nicholas and I were obliged to do a few exercises, not very regularly, and then in turn one of us would hang for a minute or two. I found this a very tedious business and took to repeating any odd verses of poetry I could remember to beguile the time. One day my mind was a blank and I could think of nothing, so that Doodles was a good deal astonished on opening the nursery door to hear me intoning the Lord's Prayer.

On another occasion Nicholas and I were at our exercises when we saw the figure of a strange lady ascending the stone stairs. We thought her gestures odd as she climbed up towards us, and fetched Doodles, who came to meet the unknown and sent us packing. It was a little while before we heard the sequel. The poor woman was an inmate of Sedgefield Asylum, some seven miles away. She was perfectly harmless, but she had an obsession that she was our mother. Doodles knew all about her, and this time she was successfully humoured back down the stairs and into the housekeeper's room where she was entertained until the asylum came to fetch her.

Another occasion had been more difficult. Arriving on foot at the front door, my mother's substitute rang the bell and informed the astonished footman, who knew nothing of the matter, that she was Lady Eden. When he appeared unconvinced she persisted: 'Oh yes I am, and there is a cab coming up the drive with my lawyer and the deeds to prove it.' The footman peered out but could see nothing, and eventually the unfortunate lady was once again invited in for a spell. We were never told whatever medical case there may have been, but my mother was always sad about it, even when 'Lady Eden' protested at some posters in a neighbouring town announcing that my mother was to open a charity bazaar, maintaining firmly to the organizers that she had never authorized the use of her name.

*

Sometimes the opening day of the holidays would happily coincide with the arrival of a new pony. On one such occasion, when I was about eight years old, joy was not unconfined. Rushing out to the stables, Nicholas and I were proudly shown by Shoebottom his latest charge, 'Tom-tit'. We were delighted with the pony, which had only one fault, its tail had been cruelly docked, and we knew how much that would bother him in the summer when we were riding near the woods. But when we asked for which of us he was intended, we could get no more than, 'You must ask Sir William.'

That evening my father told us that the pony had cost him more than he had expected and that therefore Nicholas and I must share him. I was nearly three years older than Nicholas and we were far from clear how this would work out. It did not, and led to occasional arguments and ructions.

Nicholas kept badgering his father: 'If we are sharing, which part belongs to me?' Next morning my father, who had come out to the stables to paint a water-colour of Shoebottom and 'Tom-tit', which I still have, spoke to Nicholas: 'You cannot divide the pony, but if you insist, Anthony must have the body because he is the elder, and you can have the tail.' Nicholas was near to tears as he looked ruefully at the poor stump, but afterwards we tacitly accepted that Shoebottom should arbitrate and all was well.

One Christmas holiday several years later, my brother Timothy was away from home for a while and I had the use of his bay pony, 'Well-beloved', as well as my own. This was luxury, but I was soon humbled. One day, while hounds were running, 'Well-beloved' popped over a small fence without he or I realizing how steep was the fall on the other side. We seemed to take for ever to reach the ground, but when we did we both took a purler. I was a bit dazed when I got up and began to look around for 'Well-beloved'. To my surprise and delight, I then saw, barely a hundred yards away, Mr Briggs, a senior member of the hunt who always showed us much kindness, dismounted and holding his own horse by one hand and 'Well-beloved' by the other. Still rather shaken, I ran up saying: 'Thank you so much Mr Briggs for catching "Well-beloved" for me,' and was just preparing to mount when I heard a voice saying, 'Hi, hold hard, Anthony, when you've quite finished, that's my bay mare and I'm changing horses.' Then, for the first time, I noticed a groom standing beyond Mr Briggs. It took me some weary trudging to recapture 'Well-beloved' and still longer to live the story down.

As in other spheres of interest, my father's conclusion to any incident was always on his own terms.

Soon after the First World War, I was staying at Hornby in North Yorkshire, the home of the Duke of Leeds, a medieval castle restored by Adam, then containing many treasures such as Hogarth's *The Beggar's Opera*. My host had been a friend of my father's and a frequent visitor to Windlestone in his younger days. 'Your father,' he told me, 'could afford better horses than I could and would sometimes mount me. On one occasion, however, I had a hunter of which I was rather proud and I lent him to your father, who in return lent me one of his best. Unfortunately, early in a fast run we both came down at the same fence. Your father was on his feet first, roundly abusing me for lending him such a poor horse and for putting his own good mount down.'

Though the children's ponies were very much secondary to the hunters of our elders, and even to the carriage horses, my father took a close interest in them and they were a frequent topic of conversation. One morning at breakfast I was being questioned by a cousin on leave from Sandhurst, and many years older than I, about a pony I had recently been given. This pony was lovely to look at, coal black in colour and of a highly uncertain temper. My father had christened him 'The Saint'. My cousin was inclined to pooh-pooh the pony's devilish qualities, so of course my father said, 'Take Oliver out to the stables, get Shoebottom to saddle "The Saint" and perhaps Oliver would like to try him round the yard.'

I did as I was bid, but reluctantly, for I thought my cousin much too tall for my little pony. Shoebottom quickly sized up the situation. An apparently docile pony was led out by him to be mounted. In a flash, as Oliver swung into the saddle, 'The Saint' whipped round, dashed out of the yard clattering under the stable clock, and disappeared down the drive, to Shoebottom's unrestrained delight. More than twenty minutes passed before my chastened cousin, his feet almost touching the ground on either side of the pony, regained the stable-yard.

*

My father's agent at Windlestone was now Ernest Cradock, a man of slow speech with a quiet smile and the features of a fox-terrier. We liked him, though we realized he must always be on our father's side in the end. He was a brother of Admiral Kit Cradock of Coronel fame.*

One summer afternoon my father appeared in the garden with Cradock and a pretty niece of his whom they both much admired. I admired her too. The niece and I were not yet in our early teens. 'This is pretty Mary, Anthony, and you should marry her, but mind, no children. Cradock will tell you how that is to be managed.' A giggle from the agent and bewilderment and shy looks from the victims.

Cradock was also sometimes delegated to instruct me in estate matters. One Easter, when we were not at Windlestone, I entered in my diary: 'Went over to Windles with the "old man" had lunch and tea there. Not bad fun on the whole. Went out for a walk with Mr Cradock in the afternoon to

* In 1914 Admiral Cradock, in command of a squadron of British war-ships off the South American coast, suffered a gallant if controversial defeat at Coronel against the German warships *Scharnhorst*, *Gneisenau* and others.

learn, in case I should succeed, the difference between a rainbow and a tree.'

Faithful retainers are essential ingredients to any understanding of Windlestone before the First World War. House, the butler, called Harris by my father as being a less confusing name, was young for the job, but equable, quick and popular. Having graduated as my father's valet, he was a useful guide in any household dilemma. Very severely wounded in the war, House became a cripple for life, but he never bemoaned his fate or lost interest in events. Like all who had served my father, he loved to speak of him.

It· was, I think, Woolger the discerning valet, able to gauge any mood, who told the story of the opening meet. My father had a fixed obsession that on any day when he wished especially for fine weather, the Almighty would send a downpour to vex him, much as Lord Salisbury, when Prime Minister, was convinced that bishops died to spite him. On this day the rain was true to tradition, beating down on hounds, huntsmen and loyal followers. As my father came through the front hall to join them, his eye fell on a barometer hanging on the panelled wall. He walked up to it and tapped; it read 'Set Fair'. He tapped again; it still replied 'Set Fair'. He took it off the wall, walked through the front door to the top of the flight of steps and sent it clattering down before the assembled company, saying, 'Go and see for yourself, you damned fool.'

Without question the dominant personality at Windlestone after Cradock was the head-keeper, called respectfully by us children Mr Smitton. In appearance an improved edition of King Edward VII, slow but firm of speech with a strong Scottish accent, and a master of his craft, he would without difficulty awe a bold poacher or a restless guest.

Not that there were many poachers, because an undrafted treaty was widely observed. Windlestone provided a number of hare-coursing meetings each year. As these always showed, under Smitton's watchful eye, a good supply of strong hares, they were well attended and popular. In return, poaching was not.

Partridges were plentiful at Windlestone, which claimed,

with what justification I do not know, a day's record for the North of England at that time of 169 brace to four guns, insignificant, of course, in comparison with the slaughter in the Eastern counties.

We boys were in considerable awe of Smitton, whose rules were strict and whose praise was sparing. I remember shooting my first woodcock when out with him one day, and being excusably happy about it. Smitton, however, inspected the dead bird unenthusiastically, and warned me that Sir William, who liked to eat woodcock, would not be pleased. He was right, for the bird's body was full of shot. There were some rumbles and grumbles at dinner, but happily no shafts aimed directly at me. I looked ruefully at the two feathers of my woodcock as I turned out my light that night.

Another time I had luck which I certainly did not deserve. There was a piece of marshy ground nearly two miles from the house, which was usually good for a wisp of snipe. One afternoon when we were trying our luck thereabouts, a brace of snipe got up almost at my feet. I blazed off and, to my astonishment, both fell. 'However long you live, you'll no' do that again,' was Smitton's comment. Once again he was right.

My most vivid memory of Smitton was when hounds were drawing the home coverts. Mounted on a stout cob and giving the master some wise tactical advice about the ways of Windlestone foxes, he seemed, as always, the dominant figure.

Perhaps these recollections are gilded by Smitton's inevitable appearance on any significant occasion in a shooting suit which my father insisted upon calling 'the Eden Tartan'. This was a pretty check, mainly red and brown in colour with a touch of yellow. I have no idea what its origins were, but any grown-up member of the family of either sex, or a close friend, could expect to be honoured with the gift of a suit length. Smitton was in this restricted company, while the under-keepers all wore knickerbockers and jackets of a plain dark brown material, which I secretly preferred. Nor was my taste so far out, for it was said that Mr Adam, the tailor in George Street, Hanover Square, made these clothes also.

My father did relatively little forestry in the modern sense of planting blocks of conifers for timber. There were four woodmen, however, with whom he spent much time planning the landscape. 'Commend me to the vandal with an axe' was one of his favourite sayings. My father's own axe had a raised metal 'W.E.' at the top of the haft, so that if he saw a tree he wanted felled when out alone, he could shave off a piece of the bark with his axe and then stamp it with his initials.

Once when he was tree-felling, my Uncle Robin Grey was with him. Making a wild shot, my uncle, then only a boy, cut off the tip of his nose, which hung by a thread. My father hastily clamped it back on and they set off for home. All was well except that the tip had been put back upside-down, fortunately without lasting damage to Robin's good looks.

It was not altogether unusual in those days for a country landowner to excel at his chosen pastimes. He had, after all, the opportunity and resources to perfect his prowess. My father was no exception: besides being a water-colour artist of note, he took a dominant and knowledgeable part in the management of a large estate; he was a pioneer in garden design, a good shot, a first-class man to hounds and a keen coaching whip, that is to say, a skilful conductor of a four-in-hand.

He was also an above average amateur boxer. Sometimes there would be boxing in the evenings at Windlestone. His friend and neighbour, the Duke of Leeds, used also to box, though, he insisted to me, not in my father's class. On one occasion when they were sparring, the guest, by mistake, hit his host harder than he had intended. 'The next thing I knew,' he told me, 'was that I was painfully coming-to on the floor.'

My father's interest in boxing continued after his own pugilistic days were past, and he was an early promoter of Bombardier Billy Wells. The bombardier was modest and popular as well as a beautiful boxer. He was an occasional guest at Windlestone, when sparring bouts were sometimes mounted in neighbouring mining towns. On one occasion at least the tables were pushed aside after supper in the Cavendish Hotel in London, so that the bombardier could give a sparring display. It was typical of my father's professional approach to anything which he practised himself that he would include among the toffs who made up the 'house' those of the hotel staff interested in the sport.

The idiosyncratic way of life my father led was nevertheless genuinely expressed, with intense originality and taste. As such it affected his children in various ways. Jack was impervious, his interests touched my father's out of doors only. Cheerful and open-hearted, the complex parental character seemed no more to him than that of any peppery old gentleman. Marjorie was amused and understanding, and anyway the best-loved of his children. Timothy, solitary in age between the two groups of the family was, perhaps on that account, my mother's special care. Nicholas and I, though spared some of the impact in our younger years, were often rather bewildered by what was occasionally irrational behaviour.

'You are a typical Grey,' my father used sometimes to say. I took this to mean a plodder of conventional ability and tolerable good looks, taking after my mother's family and not very exciting.

My mother had been born in India where her father, Sir William Grey, was Governor of Bengal. I was fond of my grandmother Grey, who seemed to me gentle as well as decorative. 'You are a beautiful humbug, are you not, Lady Grey?' observed my father one day at the luncheon table. My grandmother smiled, her poise unruffled. It was she who told me of my grandfather's departure for India with £200 in his pocket provided by his uncle the Prime Minister and his early years there, perhaps her way of indicating to a younger son that money and possessions are not everything. In later years I enjoyed occasional visits to grannie in her elegant house in Brunswick Square, Hove, where I was regaled with the most authentic of curries. Lady Grey lived to be ninety-six, maintaining the most perfect self-discipline and sweetness to the end.

Our mother brought a completely different element into our lives, in contrast to the Edens. Sybil Grey's beauty had captivated my father, but she now operated in a separate sphere. I suppose her way of life, her reactions and her behaviour would nowadays be considered eccentric. Then they were quite conventional, and they were appreciated. Fifty years later I still received letters from people in County Durham remembering with affection and gratitude Lady Eden and her works.

I think my mother preferred the simpler relationship which existed between donor and recipient to the more complicated one between mother and child. No doubt she often found her children mystifying, wilful or even ungrateful, though she was always conscientious about us.

Although my father almost always seemed glad to see the 'little boys' and would hail us cheerfully when we met him on our walks or rides, he never, so far as I know, took any interest in our clothes, schooling or health. I can only recall one incident when Nicholas and I were leaving the house heavily muffled up on a winter's day and he stopped us. 'Take those things off, little boys,' he said pointing at the offending mufflers. 'You will grow up with weak throats if you wear them every day.'

Virtually every aspect of our health and upbringing was naturally in our mother's care. My father paid the bills but my mother did the work, whether in correspondence or by ordering our clothes, packing our trunks for school or visiting us at middle or end of term. Dentists, oculists and doctors were all in her province; manicurists too, until my father mercifully put a stop to this extravagance.

Even so, my mother fulfilled these duties attentively. After all, there were five of us, scattered in diverse educational establishments, yet hardly ever did she fail us on any of our special occasions. I can still remember the thrill of pride I felt on supper-nights at Sandroyd, my preparatory school, when my mother would sweep in on the arm of one of the headmasters, truly beautiful.

I cannot remember my father ever being present for our Christmas holidays, still less taking an active part in arrangements for our games or reading. Yet he was conscious that there was a man's sphere as far as we boys were concerned, and perhaps felt a little guilty that he did not do what he could to fill it. At least he used to repeat often enough 'that house doth every day more wretched grow where the hen louder than the cock doth crow', whether as an apology or as a warning I do not know.

My sister Marjorie used to say that my brother Nicholas and I owed our existence to my father's unfulfilled desire for another daughter. In any event, he was fond and proud of Marjorie, he admired his wife's beauty and enjoyed the company of pretty women. To these last he could be indulgent even when they transgressed one of his cherished taboos. 'It's only pretty Fanny's way' he would say sardonically.

III

Tableaux Vivants

Although it was my father who brought his friends George Moore, Walter Sickert and Max Beerbohm to Windlestone, they all subsequently became devoted admirers of my mother:

8 King's Bench Walk, Temple.
Saturday.

Dear Lady Eden,

Before starting my novel I must write you a few lines – I miss you dreadfully. That is the worst of intimate friends, life becomes unendurable without them. I am looking forward to Windlestone. I got an invitation from Mrs Hunter to go to them on the tenth but I can't do that. I want to get three chapters done of my new book before I leave London. A novel is like a woman when you have got over the difficulties of the beginning you fall in love and she is always with you even when she is absent. A novel half-written or partly written is like a mistress, a woman gives herself and gets you.

I send you the *Saturday Review*. My letter will perhaps amuse you but to understand it you will have to read the article in last Saturday's.

Do write to me. I love to hear from you.

Yours sincerely,
George Moore

I wish you would give me a commission. Do you want anything? I love to put myself out for some people.

Wednesday.

Dear Lady Eden,

Lady Cunard has gone to Scotland for a shooting party, from

which I think she would like to escape. She could come to Windlestone any time this month, I think – twelfth, fifteenth, twentieth. Her address is Durris, Aberdeen. N. B. If you drop her a line she will let you know at once. I think she would like you to write first.

I shall send you the second chapter of *Evylyn Innes* tomorrow. You remember I showed you the first. I am crazy about my novel. I think it will be better than Esther. I can imagine that poor nun reliving in memory all the past passion of her life, and in the solitude of her cell. I shall try to bring out more distinctly than it has ever been brought out something which neither Willy nor Lady Cunard understand very deeply, but which you I think can understand – I mean *La Vie de Couvent*. Those who know what that life is know how intense and penetrating it is, how sharp are its tears. Imagine my poor Evelyn recollecting the nights on board the boat, the sailors have got up a concert among themselves and Evelyn the most beautiful voice in Europe sings one night under the stars. How acute the memory of that song would be in her, more than when she sang in the opera houses, how sharpened her memory would be by the grey convent monotony – no more lovers, never another, never again would a man take her in his arms saying 'dearest'. How thin the Christ would grow on the wall, how far away, and how full and luminous would the blue Mediterranean nights seem, bewitched by memory. How wonderful is memory, memory is in literature what *clair obscure* is in painting. Writers make too little use of memory, recollection! How extraordinary is recollection. . .

I have no gifts as a letter writer; I cannot improvise and it is difficult to imagine anyone making copies of his letters to his intimate friends. What did Willie think of my article on Ellis Roberts? He has sent me some notes for my book, they are very funny – he amuses me more than anyone – his artless naturalness tickles me.

Always sincerely yours,
George Moore

Boodle's, St James's Street, s.w.
Thursday.

Dear Lady Eden,

Well, you are quite right, the verses I sent you are mediocre. But I did not know you were so good a judge. I thought that they were pretty well, that they might pass. You judge them better. . .

I liked Windlestone very much. I was in excessive health and spirits and enjoyed myself to the top of my bent. But from over-eating or eating something that did not suit me I fell ill and could not go out hunting. Sir William offered me your cob. Don't be angry I should have taken the greatest care of him.

I send you my fresh poem. I think you will – I have just dis-covered that the stupid boy has brought back the wrong paper. It is too late to send for another; I should miss the post.

I am very busy composing my new novel – *The Nun*. As soon as I have got it into shape I'll write the article. I asked you to come for a walk on the boulevard; I had a reason, but you were always engaged with other admirers.

Always yours,
George Moore

Sybil Eden enjoyed the woman's prerogative of those days: she was unpunctual. This was a form of being spoilt which occasionally entailed discomfort for herself as well as for others. During our foreign travels, trains could be missed with impunity, but I remember one fine summer's day when we crested the hill in our carriage above some French Channel port, Dieppe perhaps, and there as a vignette below us we saw our boat chugging purposefully into a calm open sea. As my mother was a bad sailor and we had to take the chance of weather on another day, this was indeed *une journée manquée*.

My father was inevitably a victim of this unpunctuality. On the silver wedding day of my parents, which was also Jack's coming-of-age, when the time arrived for the opening ceremonies at Windlestone, the participants were assembled on the terrace before the front door, my father, we children, family and friends, all except my mother. My father had answered the pressmen's questions about his married life and Jack's future and was then heard to add: 'I have been married twenty-five years and I have spent five of them waiting on the doorstep for my wife.'

The celebrations were a grand affair and lasted three days. On the first day there was a large garden party for friends and neighbours from miles around and, despite the slower and limited transport, difficulties of travel at that time seemed to be more readily braved. The second day was for tenant farmers and centred round a luncheon in a large marquee, where beer was drunk which had been laid down at Jack's birthday, but we boys were not offered any. There seemed to be a great number of people, many of them strangers, for some came from distant parts of the estate, including West Auckland farms of which I knew little. But the atmosphere was relaxed, even intimate, as among a closed company of friends. The inevitable speeches followed of which I can only remember a farmer drawing the loudest applause with the statement: 'Whatever the weather, ye know every one of ye that when ye return home there will be no leaking roof in your house.' This stuck in my mind only because I could not conceive at the time how the speaker could have expected otherwise; which shows how much I had to learn of the art of public-speaking.

The third day was for all those employed on the estate, outdoors and in, and this I enjoyed the best, for then I encountered many cronies, the men and women on whom the smooth functioning of the Windlestone estate depended. They in turn knew they could count on my father to see that they were well housed and well paid, and on my mother to make sure that they were looked after in sickness and adversity. If they considered that my parents were fulfilling their side of the bargain, they would anticipate that they and their descendants would work on the estate for generations, as indeed many of them had.

It all seemed so permanent; the same family had been established at this same site for four centuries. Why should it end in any of our lifetimes? As we celebrated Jack's gay coming-of-age, in the brilliant summer of 1911, none of us had an inkling of the holocaust to come.

*

My mother was responsible for the amateur theatricals which took place every Christmas holiday. They were usually enacted in the East Hall where the Burlinsons, father and son, the skilled estate carpenters, would set up a stage and any scenery that might be needed. Our earliest efforts were *tableaux vivants*, a type of entertainment which seemed to me to place the maximum strain on actors and audience alike. Much rehearsal was needed to perfect one *tableau* which was then displayed for perhaps two or three minutes, after which the audience had to twiddle its thumbs while the actors changed and the props were moved around for the next picture. However, this pastime did have the advantage of allowing my mother to appear in a series of costumes and poses which enabled her classic features to be studied at leisure by the spectators. For this purpose her children came in handy. I can remember in one evening taking part in two of her favourite *tableaux*, *The Murder of Rizzio* and *The Mother of the Gracchi.*

Later we became more ambitious and began to stage plays. One year, for some reason which I cannot recall, the site was changed to the small village school which my grandfather had built at Rushyford. The play was *Alice in Wonderland* and my brother Timothy, generally considered the most histrionically gifted of the family, was the Mad Hatter, and I the Dormouse. It was fun to dress up in costume and mask, and pleasantly lazy to have so few words to learn; but I wasn't sure by the end that these advantages were not outweighed by the pinches the poor Dormouse had to suffer.

All my mother's friends were expected to play their part:

13 Robert Street, Cumberland Market, N.W.

1 January 1898.

Dear Lady Eden,

No, ma'am, I will not forget to come on Thursday or Friday.

I went this morning to the Strand and found Lucy or French's shop shut. But that is no matter. I have bought a moustache and a complexion for the part and spirit gum to stick the moustache on with.

I will make it my affair to get the paper I saw and bring it with me.

You must have had a day of it and atop of all the Christmas duties! I shall get up as a kind of amateur McCullough and endeavour to persuade you as much as possible to make a duty of occasional lapses from or excursions from duty. I think this call to the drama is a very good thing for you – in fact nothing but my belief in it as a change for you from dusting and tying your parcels would induce me at my time of life to compromise my respectable and studious reputation by gadding over the country play-acting with ladyships! I wonder if you have the slightest idea what devotion such an upheaval from all my habits implies!

> Ever your *bien dévoué*
> *Walter Sickert*

13 Robert Street, Cumberland Market, N.W.

Dear Lady Eden,

What a beast of a man! 'Robert' I hasten to explain! How I study! Can a man give a greater proof of his devotion than to paint his face red and gum on a moustache and make an ass of himself for the lady of his worship? *Je vous demande un peu!*

After my bullying Robin I am in a terror not to be letter perfect. It is really quite delightful to be coming back. . .

. I had a most interesting evening with Moore who is crazy about the Millais Exhibition and in love with Lady Randolph Churchill.

I have done a lot of work with accumulated Windlestone energy and spirits and deep in the revival of tempera-painting.

Max Beerbohm is enchanted to be coming. His sister has just got through a very serious operation and I wasn't sure he would be able to leave till today. The little donkey is engaged to an excellent young woman who is a super in his brother's theatre! I wish you would fill Windlestone with eligible sirens anxious to marry a penniless *Saturday Review*er!

> Believe me, dear Lady Eden,
> Ever your unconverted,
> *Walter Sickert*

I have got a sitting tomorrow from George Bernard Cocksure, as I call him, the G.B.S. of the *Saturday Review* and *Vanity Fair*.

When I think of my mother it is of her sitting at the writing-table in what was in those days called a boudoir. On her left through the window the garden sloped down to the west, with the woods a dark mass on the horizon. This boudoir was my mother's creation; with mauve as the predominant colour, it always gave the impression of being crowded. Every chair was covered with packets of papers concerning her good works and the many small tables were dotted with bibelots.

She seemed to write about twenty letters a day, most of them concerned with her charities or with the welfare of army reservists. No one apparently thought of using a secretary in those days. These reservists, most of them old soldiers from the Boer War, would often turn up and be interviewed by my mother and given help or money. I remember the tattered bits of paper which the old soldiers would produce as evidence of their service.

My father would tease my mother sometimes about her 'innumerable reservists', but he never attempted to interfere and I suspect secretly approved, even though they had their share in the recurrent crises over the housekeeping bills. My mother also made frequent visits to near or distant parts of the estate, usually driving herself in her pony carriage, taking food and other more substantial gifts from home to the sick and aged. After Sunday church we would drive round to some of the more ancient pensioners who were her particular care. Nicholas and I were rather shy of these visitations, the least intimidating of the old widow ladies being Mrs Richelieu who gave us coloured eggs at Easter.

My mother naturally redoubled her efforts at Christmas. After my father's death, the home farm being then let, my brother Timothy who had succeeded to the estate received a shattering bill from the local butcher for prime sirloins which had been distributed to all the tenants. Although there was no longer any home-produced beef, my mother did not see why the tenants should go without.

Another activity of which my father firmly approved was my mother's effort to raise funds to build a cottage hospital at Bishop Auckland. In those days there was no hospital between Durham and Darlington, eighteen miles apart, and the West Durham coalfield had need of help nearer at hand. My mother would beg indefatigably from her wealthier friends and neighbours. 'I hate begging,' she confessed in one of these appeals which brought the fair retort, 'If you hate begging, I hate giving,' softened by a handsome cheque.

At length enough money had been collected for the site to be bought and the hospital to be built. Then came the question of who should perform the opening ceremony. My mother wrote off to her old friend Lord Rosebery, who accepted forthwith. Although Rosebery had resigned from the leadership of the Liberal Party a few years before, local rumour had it that my father was to join the Liberals, a lesson in the smoke without fire of political tittle-tattle.

Some time later, when the hospital was in full use, the carriage journey to Bishop Auckland, four miles away, became one more drive we used to take. My mother really loved her good works and much of her life was devoted to them.

*

Trains played the essential part in my childhood which motor cars do today; clean, shining, painted trains, run with pride and efficiency, a civilized and comfortable form of transport. As a very young child I can remember our being met by carriage at Bradbury station, with its wooden buildings and benevolent stationmaster, where the express from the South was stopped for us. By the time I was a schoolboy the hay store at Windlestone had been converted into garages for my father's motor cars, and we would then be driven the ten miles to Darlington station where we boarded the south-bound express, but further up the line to London. These frequent journeys to and from school were in themselves an event, experienced with joy or regret. 'Hail to thee, Daddie's property' we would cry out as we crossed the estate boundary on the way home and more ruefully, 'Farewell to thee, Daddie's property' in the contrary direction. Railways were regarded with awe and interest by us children and the railway staffs as friends who could be kind enough to explain to us some of the mysteries. My father encouraged us in this, so that it seemed natural that on his last journey home the railway porters at Darlington asked to be allowed to carry his coffin themselves from the train to the waiting hearse.

As with all other ventures, my father embarked on the age of the combustion engine with style. He had two Benz, a limousine in the country and a smaller brougham-type in London. Both these, and a Siddeley as auxiliary at Windlestone, were painted yellow, as the carriages had been, and the bodies were made by Hooper. Adolf, the Austrian chauffeur, was universally popular with the women for his waltzing, with the men for his driving and mechanical skills and with everyone for his manners. I was distressed, when in France during the war, to learn that he had been interned.

IV

Golden Seasons

From as early as I can remember, my father had a flat at No. 12b Waterloo Place. I recall this mistily but happily, for we always enjoyed our brief stays there, usually on the way to or from boarding school. It was something of a climb to reach the flat, but once there we were spoilt by a welcoming house-keeper, a prestigious cook and a kindly parlourmaid.

In the summer months we would usually take a house in London for the Season. Aged between six and eight years old, I had mixed feelings about these moves. Sometimes I liked the houses and our schoolroom and I remember with par-ticular favour 11 Bruton Street and a house in Grosvenor Crescent. It was outside the latter that the family was one morning piled into a new motor car, this time a Napier, solemnly photographed and then told to get out again. I thought this a very disappointing arrangement, I had anticipated a thrilling drive.

The less satisfactory part of our London visits were the *cours* which Nicholas and I had to attend for our instruction. Our French *cours* was conducted by Monsieur Roche, I think at the Asquith house in Cavendish Square. We were a glum band of small children and shy of Monsieur Roche. Not so our host's gaily precocious daughter, Elizabeth. Apt to be late for our lessons, she tripped in one day bearing a single red rose. Dropping a deep curtsey, she enunciated clearly, '*Pardonnez moi, Monsieur Roche,*' and laid the rose before him. Our teacher received the offering quizzically.

Dancing classes were also prescribed from time to time when we were in London. I detested them, mainly I think because, although the polka and the waltz were by now fashionable, we, for some mysterious reason, had always to begin with the minuet. The bowing and scraping and mincing round in circles were singularly unsuited to little boys. It was not until the Charleston of the twenties that I really enjoyed dancing.

On one occasion during the term at Sandroyd, when I was in sick bay for some childish ailment, my mother paid an unexpected visit to the school. It turned out that her purpose was to tell me that my sister Marjorie was engaged to be married. 'Guess to whom?' my mother asked. 'Guy,' I answered without hesitation. My mother was rather taken aback, but the truth was that Guy Brooke had been the only one of my sister's admirers to imprint his personality on Nicholas and myself by reason of his charm and attentions.

As the wedding day approached I disgraced myself. A few days before I was due to go back to Sandroyd for the summer term, I developed measles. We were then already installed in the Asquith's house in Cavendish Square which we had taken that year, the Asquith family having presumably moved to No. 10 Downing Street. There was nothing to be done except to conceal me on the top floor behind a barrier of disinfectant. It was a dreary period, for I saw hardly anyone and felt very ill. There was some reward, however, as the wedding drew nearer, when I was finally pronounced free of infection, though not allowed to attend the festivities. Wrapped up in countless blankets I was taken down to the drawing room to see the display of presents. Particularly impressive were a large silver bowl adorned with the stars and stripes, a gift from Maryland, with which the family had connections, and a large pile of umbrellas. I could not imagine what Guy and Marjorie would do with so many; nor, no doubt, could they.

Best treat of all was the dazzling sight of Marjorie in her wedding dress when she came up to my attic to show herself to me before leaving for the church. This made up for everything; it had never occurred to me until then how beautiful she was.

*

It must have been about this time that the choice of a public school was mooted. It was not so easily determined. As a little boy I had expressed wild enthusiasm for the Royal Horse Artillery, first inspired by their brilliant uniforms and display at the Royal Military Tournament. This attachment came to be accepted to the point of Cheltenham being proposed as suitable for the future education of a would-be gunner. At some stage I developed doubts, which were strongly fortified by Timothy who wanted me to join him at Eton. When his house tutor offered a vacancy, this tilted the scale. For this conclusion I am grateful in retrospect; advanced mathematics must always have been beyond my grasp.

Though I never pretended to like school and my years there were far from the happiest in my life, the independence and freedom of choice which Eton encouraged were some compensation. I preferred Greek to Latin and French to either, while rowing and sculling on the river were a constant enjoyment.

*

I do not know what caused my father to abandon Waterloo Place, maybe the lease ran out, but at about the time I went to Eton he bought a house in Old Queen Street. Certainly we were there in 1911, for the leads, so easy of access from the long dining-room windows, gave us a front seat view of troops and guns going by to take part in the Coronation procession. I had just invested in my first camera, a 3A Kodak, and the very amateur consequences still exist.

To me the house was grand but sombre and mainly associated with journeys to and from school. Perhaps that is why the dining room is clearest in my memory with its Waterford glass on the sideboard faintly shimmering in the dimly lit setting. It was here, too, that I had high tea with Timothy and Charles des Graz, then captain of our house, before catching our train back to Eton. In the midst of our meal, glum for me but perhaps falsely talkative for my seniors, a noisy shouting match suddenly broke out next door between my father and Jack, probably about Jack's allowance, for he was a generous spender, which ended in Jack storming out and slamming the front door. Timothy looked embarrassed and des Graz raised one eyebrow.

It was nearer August 1914 that there was also controversy between father and son about Jack's engagement to Pamela Fitzgerald. My father never spoke to me of this and maybe it was exaggerated by others. My mother appeared to think it was because Pamela was a Roman Catholic, but this seemed unlikely to me in view of my father's frequently expressed agnostic opinions.

I never saw Pamela until after Jack had been killed when she journeyed to Windlestone for the memorial service which was held in the chapel. I admired her grace and elegance and her fair beauty and felt an almost reverential respect for her as the girl Jack had loved. When the time came to return to London it fell out that I was to drive to Darlington with Pamela to catch the express. 'Yes,' commented my mother sharply, 'and then you can flirt all the way to London.' I was shocked, because Pamela was for me on a pedestal, and angry because my mother had not understood this. Pamela married later in the war, her husband was killed and she died in the influenza epidemic of 1918.

*

My father's last change in his London home came only a year or two after our move into Old Queen Street. This time into a smaller house more after my taste, in Duke Street, St James's. I have a water-colour of part of the drawing room there with Ming animal figures which are now on the mantelpiece of our dining room at Alvediston. I thought the Duke Street house cosy and comfortable after the manner of Waterloo Place, and I liked its bachelor atmosphere. On an easel in the drawing room stood *La Première Danseuse*, my favourite Degas. My father made a copy of this painting, and many years later I received a letter of inquiry from the United States about a Degas which had been owned by Sir William Eden. There appeared to be some doubt about the painting; was it the original, or had my father had a copy made? He would have been gratified that there should have been any uncertainty.

As his health began to fail my father found the stairs in

Duke Street too much for him. The house backed conveniently on to the Cavendish Hotel, which we children would sometimes visit under Mrs Lewis's now famous sovereignty. My father knocked a hole through the dividing wall into the hotel and would occasionally dine there on his now rare journeys to London. When his health grew worse, on what proved to be his last visit, he moved into a ground-floor room in the hotel which looked on to a quiet courtyard. It was there that Nicholas and I saw him for the last time.

*

The summer of 1914 at Eton, as I turned seventeen, is vivid in my mind. Sarajevo sounded ominously even in our schoolboy ears, for we were encouraged to take an interest in public affairs. Years later, I remember watching with my former tutor a house game of the school's admirable brand of football in which my elder son was playing. I remarked on the appearance and manners of the boys I had met that day; they seemed to be an improvement on my generation. My tutor shook his head: 'They may be better mannered,' he replied, 'they may even be a nicer lot of fellows, but they are not so well educated.'

There had been plenty of talk too, during earlier holidays, of Germany's intentions and the challenge by that country's sea-power. My eldest brother was in the Twelfth Lancers, then stationed at Norwich, my youngest was a cadet leaving Osborne for Dartmouth. My second brother, Timothy, was to try for the Diplomatic Service and was in Germany to complete his knowledge of the language. My mother's only brother, Robin Grey, was a pilot in the Royal Flying Corps, and we had been to see him fly, though I have a clearer view of Uncle Robin in flying suit and gloves and helmet than I have of his startlingly fragile machine. Our only uncle was popular with the family. Inheriting with my mother her family's good looks, he had also been something of a rolling stone, his activities ranging from growing oranges in Florida, which failed, to an admiration for Dame Nellie Melba, reputedly more successful.

Lord Roberts's campaign for greater preparedness was frequently discussed in the family, and I had been to see *An*

Englishman's Home more than once. The theme was the feck-less Englishman who will not make ready, preferring the golf course to the Territorials, so that his country is at the mercy of the thinly disguised German invader when he lands and the Englishman's home comes under fire. We had even been sufficiently sophisticated to be sceptical whether the mixed bag of British soldiers and sailors could really have arrived in time for that rescue in the last act.

The family had relations and friends concerned with every development in the events of that summer, so that without being in any sense jingo we were very much aware of the growing menace of war. Even so, we made our mistakes like others. For instance, Timothy was allowed to stay in Germany and was caught and interned there, adding in consequence to the cares and sorrows my poor mother was soon to have to bear.

Most of this foreboding was thrust into the background for the Eton and Harrow match in July. It all seemed gaiety, sunshine and good food. The river at Eton had been a grow-ing pleasure that summer. Races had been enjoyable despite the training, and the occasional excursion up the river to our club at Queen's Eyot was always fun. In spite of which I looked forward immensely to my long-leave which began with a luncheon with my brother Jack at the Cavalry Club. This was a proud but fearsome interlude, for Jack was nine years older than I and had been abroad with his regiment in India and South Africa for many years, so that we did not know each other well. Jack was very much my hero but I was in-timidated by his altered and dashing appearance which included a new moustache and a monocle. I was also over-awed by the large club room and the many friends who came up to ask about regimental polo prospects for that weekend, to the point where my words would hardly come at all. I suspect that we were both relieved when the time came to pay the bill and leave in his Austro-Daimler for Lords.

During an interval in the game, Jack introduced me to a fellow officer in his regiment who had, he told me, scored a century for both Harrow and Cambridge at Lords. I was as much impressed by this heroic feat as shocked by this double achievement for the wrong cause. Within six months both men had been killed in action.

The next afternoon I went with my mother to watch Jack play in the final of the Subaltern's cup, I suppose at Hurlingham. This was an exciting summer for the Twelfth Lancers, for they won both the Regimental cup and the Subaltern's cup, a conjunction of events which did not occur every day of the year, Jack explained, excusing himself later for not going to dinner and the play with us. I understood little of the game and my chief impression was of the large crowd dominated by the hats like laden trays of the gaily dressed women. It was a brilliant scene worthy of Renoir.

One incident concerned us; Jack took what seemed a nasty fall. I felt my mother hold her breath beside me and it was a moment before fellow officers in our stand could reassure her. However, the game was won and all was well on that sunny afternoon, the last when I was to see Jack.

*

In the closing days of July the Eton College Officers Training Corps was in camp together with contingents from other schools. Years later Hitler was to cite those activities to me as proof of the military training of British youth. They hardly deserved such renown, even though the light grey uniforms with their pale blue facings did give our school contingent a superficially Germanic look.

In that year at camp the talk was all of war. Would there be one, would our country be involved, how long would it last and, only occasionally because the contingency seemed comparatively remote, should we personally have any part in it? The general expectation was that the war if it came would be brief and over in a matter of six weeks. There were no Kitcheners amongst us.

While each boy had his individual angle, the general mood was not one of eagerness for war. There was excitement, due mainly to novelty, for the Boer War had ended twelve years before, and was a dim memory at our age. There was no conception at all of what the war would really be like. Our military literature, as far as we had any, belonged to the turn of the century with such books as *The Defence of Duffer's Drift*.

That year the training seemed more strenuous than usual, two all-day exercises and one all-night one and occasional marches, but we managed to glean news all the same. Most evenings Ranger and I would find time to walk down to the camp gates where the latest editions of the newspapers were on sale, and there we would walk up and down discussing their contents. Ranger was the sergeant of our section, he was also quietly amusing and a brilliant scholar. It was told of him that he once secured ninety-nine marks out of a hundred in an examination on a Greek unseen, only to be greeted by our tutor with. 'You fool, you fool, why did you drop that odd mark?'

On one of our evening quests, Ranger and I read of the Russian mobilization. This seemed to darken our world and we looked glumly at each other. Curiously enough that news gave me the first sense of foreboding I had, and I can feel it still. Even then we were not sure, but our hopes were ill-founded for they rested mainly on the Germans by-passing Belgium. Against this was a growing conviction that we must be involved anyway, even if only at sea at first.

When we got back to our lines and were discussing this new event with others, our platoon commander came up. He was a popular master and we told him our anxious thoughts, but he would have none of them: 'There won't be any war,' he said, 'the City would never allow it. Even if fighting did break out, it couldn't last more than a few days, the money would run out.' This young man was to do brilliantly in the war and to command a battalion in France. His view was by no means uncommon at that time.

A few mornings later our orderly corporals aroused us with the order: 'Pack your kit bags. We parade within the hour to march to the station and entrain for Windsor.' It was soon evident what had happened. Our adjutant, our instructors and, most serious of all, our army cooks had all vanished in the night. The British mobilization order had gone out. An hour later we marched from our deserted camp to the strains of 'Tipperary', which was a pre-war tune.

For some reason which I never entirely understood, my mother had taken a large furnished house in Sussex that year. It was not a sympathetic house and the furnishing and pictures were ugly. I was hardly surprised to learn that, though my father had been to stay, he showed no wish to come back. I can only suppose that my mother had made these arrangements earlier in the year because my father was very ill and she thought that the invasion of my younger brother Nicholas and myself at Windlestone for the whole holidays might be too much for him.

As it was, Nicholas and I spent a few disjointed weeks in Sussex. The news of Timothy in Germany was inevitably vague and scrappy. Jack entrained for France while Uncle Robin flew off there with his squadron. Except for Nicholas, I was closer to my sister Marjorie than to any other member of the family. Though Marjorie was the eldest and I only number four, this had been so for as long as I could remember. Perhaps a reason was that my elder brothers were often away at school, whereas my sister, while she disappeared to learn German in Dresden or Italian in Florence, was often at home when they were not.

However it came about, I had a deep affection for Marjorie and was always happy with her. It was therefore an added sadness in these weeks to learn that she was leaving to join a hospital train in France and that I should only see her rarely. Years later, when Winston Churchill and I were colleagues in the Second World War, he often spoke to me of seeing Marjorie standing at the door of that hospital train at Poperinghe, during the battle of Ypres. In her nurse's uniform, 'She looked beautiful as an angel' he would say.

V

The Silent Garden

I liked to be alone with my father. He would then usually treat me as an equal, rather than embarrass me as a witness or butt. However, my last visit to Windlestone in his lifetime was a tragic experience. There were no guests in the house, nor children, and I had never known it without both. It was the early autumn of 1914, the rooms and the passages were hushed and sombre as though someone were dead in the house already, my father hating noise. 'The merry, merry plough-boy goes whistling o'er the lea,' he used to quote, 'to those who don't like whistling what a nuisance he must be.'

My father was himself by this time scarcely mobile, a wheel-chair in the house and a bath-chair in the garden was the best he could do. At times his thoughts wandered, but more often he was mentally alert and very good company. I particularly enjoyed the peregrinations through the garden when Watson, the large and equable head-gardener, and perhaps Cradock also, would accompany us, for my father liked an audience.

First there would be instruction upon 'the garden without flowers' of which he loved to speak. This, he would explain, must mean not only the abolition of pudding beds, which were anathema, but laying down long stretches of mown lawn with only statues and poplars for decoration. There was one each of these on the north and south side of the main flower garden. The making of the southern one had presented no great problem, only the removal of the flower-beds, their replacement by Italian *bambini* on pedestals and, at the west end by the gate into the wood, the insertion into the wall of a pretty Venetian fountain.

Bourke, an engaging Irishman, was the provider of much of this Italian statuary and well-heads. 'Truth lies at the bottom of the well,' he used to say, 'and I am the damnedest liar that ever lived.'

The northern stretch of this garden without flowers presented a more complicated problem, for along its whole stretch ran greenhouses facing south. I can remember little of these except for one house near the western edge of the range. Against its back wall grew a tall and spreading grey-leaved creeper with a bright violet-blue flower. Lassiandra Macrantha it was then called, and I found the plant again many years later in Madeira.

The solution to the intrusive greenhouses had been found by lifting them over the wall and setting them well back from it, some of them against a farther wall, with two new narrow connecting houses, whose outer door gave on to the grassed walk, now also without flowers. As we followed my father in his chair, he was soon discussing an inscription by Septimius Severus which had been found in the neighbourhood and was now let into the wall, seeming quite at home among Bourke's more recent finds.

Next, my father would take a turn to the left into the flower-garden and begin to talk of colour, the beds on either side being filled with lavender bushes interspaced with salvia blue-beard. His first choice was for blues and greys, but white was not excluded. I can also remember a bed in a more remote part of the garden where tiger lilies had the place to themselves against a cotoneaster hedge. Even a dash of the usually ostracized red was allowed to persist in a few climbing plants of tropaeolum on some of the long established yew hedges.

My father loved to paint water-colours of his garden up to the time of his last illness, and I am sure that he designed and laid out his borders and his schemes of colour with the pictures which he was going to paint in mind. In this sense it was a painter's garden.

Dinner depended much upon my father's health of the moment. Gout ranking high among his ailments as it had among his father's, he could drink no wine. I was occasionally allowed a glass of claret from a cellar which Mr Berry kept admirably stocked, encouraging me in a taste for that wine which my wife and I share happily to this day. My father would ask about Eton, but without any real interest. He had disliked his own school days and would speak of the cruelty of the beatings he suffered. I was even told, though not by him, that he and young Lambton had run away together and found their way home to County Durham, only to be returned at once to duty.

Though my father would sometimes boast of his children's modest school distinctions, one could never be sure of his reaction. I once won a divinity prize at Eton of which he took a dim view. I explained that this was really for Greek Testament and had nothing to do with reading or listening to sermons. But he was not to be comforted and all those holidays I was introduced sadly as 'my son who is going into the Church', or sometimes as 'my son who is going to be a bishop'.

My father would sometimes question me about the ride I had taken that day. Perhaps he would have asked me to look at some farm where he was making alterations, or some copse which had been recently planted, and want a report which had better be precise and detailed. This was excellent training though I did not know it at the time. My daily round was much the same, usually a ride in the morning by myself and in the afternoon occasionally with Smitton, but more often with an under-keeper, dog and game-bag after partridges and hares. All of which would have been the perfect holiday for a boy just seventeen, but for the shadow which the war and my father's illness had thrown over all at Windlestone. There were enlistments, anxious discussions about the future and uncertainty everywhere.

After dinner we would return to my father's sitting-room where he would stretch out on the sofa and talk for a while, sometimes reciting for many minutes from a book he loved before dozing off. It took me an evening or two to work out what to do then. The first time, when I picked up a *Yorkshire Post* neatly folded at my side and opened it to read, there came an oath from the sofa, my father complaining that the crackling of the newspaper had woken him. So I worked out a better technique. I had a book at my side, or if I wanted to read a newspaper, would open it in advance and have to be content with the page I had chosen.

Our talk was sometimes of his pictures, but more often of books, family or the war, the last two vaguely and uncertainly. My father used to say that the world had only improved in three respects in his lifetime. Anaesthetics had been discovered, antiseptics had been introduced and torture was no longer used in any civilized country. He would have been sadly undeceived about the last, had he been alive today.

I had always envied my father his memory, which was not only for poems or plays he enjoyed, but even for long extracts from a favoured novel like *Catriona*. This could have been a gift inherited from his grandfather, of whom it was told that having been present at a school speech-day when a lengthy prologue was spoken in Latin, the college authorities were surprised to read it word for word in a newspaper the next day. Inquiry revealed that Sir Frederick had memorized the prologue, which had impressed him, and had given it to the newspaper.

No doubt this gift of memory helped him to make a contribution to our country's social history. Frederick Morton Eden's *State of the Poor* is a detailed account of the living and working conditions in many English parishes at the close of the eighteenth century. As such it is still a classic. Having also founded the Globe Insurance Company, had his lovely wife painted by Romney, and been the subject of a family ghost story, Sir Frederick played his part in the Eden annals:

On 14 November 1809, Sir F. M. Eden died of gout in Pall Mall, the Carlton Club now covering the site of the house which he then occupied.

Sir Frederick had for some time had apartments at Hampton Court Palace, consisting of the first floor rooms over the Western Gateway, with others *en suite*. On the night that he died in London, his eldest daughter, Mariana, then a girl of about sixteen, having no reason to suppose that her father was seriously ill, was at home, as usual, in those apartments. Her bedroom was on the entresol storey, where the window came down to the floor. When she had gone into her bedroom and had got into bed, she told her maid to pull up the blind, that the bright moon might shine into the room. On raising the blind the maid cried out in a terrified voice, 'Oh, Miss, there is Sir Frederick in his coffin.' Miss Eden jumped out of bed, and sent the girl out of the room. She then herself saw the head of a coffin close to the window, and her father lying in it dead. The next morning the news reached her that he had died in the night. This is the account of the strange occurrence which she herself gave to her nephew, Frederick Morton Eden, the eldest son of the late Bishop of Moray and Ross.*

The days of my last visit to Windlestone in my father's life-time were soon gone, as is the way with the holidays when one is young. I saw him alive only once or twice more, in his last illness in London in the following February. He told Nicholas and me, the 'little boys', as he still called us, that we could have his guns: 'I shall not need them any more.' I only heard him express regret once, that he could no longer hold a brush to the paper. His eyes saddened and he looked towards us, but without seeing us any longer.

Although my father spent so much of his life on horseback, I think of him on foot, returning from one of his frequent walks with Cradock to some wood or farm, hazel stick in hand, or sitting on a bench in the garden with his brother Morton or some other guest.

*

These were miserable months for my mother. My brother Jack was killed on a cavalry patrol near Ypres in October 1914; my father died in the following February; and her brother, Robin Grey, had been shot down in his aeroplane and taken prisoner. He tried repeatedly to escape, once almost reaching the Dutch frontier. He was recaptured and was soon to suffer solitary confinement for being a cousin of Edward Grey, then Foreign Secretary.

During the first autumn of the war the corps at Eton came to life as something that mattered, and there were special camps in the holidays in the following spring for those of us who would soon be joining up.

Meanwhile I was becoming increasingly impatient to have

* *Some Historical notes of the Eden Family*, privately printed, 1907.

done with schooling. As an intelligent diversion, my house tutor, Mr E. L. Churchill, had arranged Greek 'extra books' for two or three of us, which meant reading the plays with a kindly clergyman, a gentle scholar, This was my introduction to the Loeb classics. When we parted he said to me ruefully: 'Now you can take pleasure in the plays, but by the time the war is over you will have forgotten much and will not wish to read them in Greek again.' That proved sadly true.

It was a habit of my tutor to make a round of the boys' rooms before lights out. Sometimes this was perfunctory, at others he would discuss some topic which was on his mind. I liked my tutor though I was a little frightened of him. I learnt later that he had defended me in one or two letters in answer to some doubting queries from my mother about my work; and the inscription in the leaving book which he gave me was, according to my brother Timothy, unusual if not unprecedented in its generosity.

There was one occasion when he cut me down to size without changing my mind. Our house had won the Aquatic cup in the summer of 1915 and Churchill, who was now eagerly casting next year's rowing horoscope, remarked, 'I think you should stroke the house four.' Normally I should have been excited and flattered at the prospect. As it was, I could only gape and eventually utter, 'But, sir, haven't you had a letter from my mother?' 'No. Is there any reason why I should have?' 'Yes sir, my mother promised to write to you about my leaving.' 'Leaving!' exclaimed my tutor. 'Why on earth should you do that?' 'To go to the war.' 'Oh you fool,' came the retort as much in sorrow as in anger. 'You won't be any use at the war, but you could be some help in the house four.'

The headmaster was a more remote personality. Edward Lyttelton was respected by the boys, though he puzzled them. I was not enough of a classical scholar nor enough of a rogue to know him at all well. Yet when I went to take leave, he spoke as though we had long been friends and I enjoyed our talk though its end was unexpected. He was regretful but not reproachful about my leaving early, and gave me my book which was the poems of Virgil. He added: 'When the war is over you will come down to have luncheon with me.'

'Thank you, sir, I should like that very much,' I replied and meant it. 'And after luncheon,' continued the headmaster, 'we will go out into the garden and read Virgil together.' It was part of Lyttelton's charm to be himself always and this trait appealed to us boys even if we were no more conscious of it than he was.

VI

Yeomen

Naturally there was much talk amongst us at Eton as to which regiment we should try to join. The Coldstream were at Windsor and an easy contact. The Grenadier Guards had a firm and loyal following, and there were always Green-jackets around. For a few of the most adventurous, the Royal Flying Corps was the first choice, but this was still very much a *corps d'élite*. Early in 1915 the casualties began to be heavy in every regiment, as we knew from our deeply moving intercession services in College chapel every week.

My sister Marjorie had been active with suggestions from her hospital train. An early call from Jack to join him in the Twelfth Lancers having lost its meaning with his death, Marjorie had advocated the Warwickshire Royal Horse Artillery which her husband, Guy Brooke, had commanded in peace-time. As that battery was already on active service in France, its commanding officer wisely decided that there was no room in his unit for an untrained schoolboy of seventeen, whose only qualification was that he could ride.

Marjorie next called in aid Guy's uncle, Sidney Greville, and by the early summer of 1915 all appeared set through his efforts for the preparation of papers and an interview with the Grenadier Guards. Then took place one of those accidents which can change the whole course of life. The author of the main event was Kitchener, then Secretary of State for War, and myself, an insignificant cog in the wheel.

It came about in this way. A number of yeomanry regiments were already in existence, keen and of first-class material. As the war was developing, it seemed unlikely that there would be a call for more cavalry or yeomanry units.

Yet it was important to tap the yeomen of England, in this instance the sons of owner or tenant farmers, in a call for volunteers. Wisely, Kitchener or the War Office decided that such an appeal was more likely to succeed if accompanied by a promise that the yeomen who volunteered should serve together as one unit. The Northern Command was chosen as the area for the experiment and Lord Feversham, then commanding the Yorkshire Hussars and until recently a Member of Parliament for a North Riding constituency, as the first commanding officer of the new battalion. It was to be known as the Yeoman Rifles and to form part of the King's Royal Rifle Corps (Sixtieth Rifles).

Charlie Feversham had married some years earlier Guy's sister, Marjorie Greville, known to her friends as Queenie. To me she was lovelier than her mother, the spectacular Daisy Warwick, with huge heavy-lidded eyes, a small nose and the fashionable rosebud mouth. Nicholas and I had first fallen under her spell when, alone among a house full of guests, she had taken the trouble to inspect and praise our guinea pigs hidden away in a remote and rough piece of garden known as the laundry green, which she did not hesitate to penetrate.

Queenie and my sister Marjorie were the closest of friends. Once, when they were very much younger and before Marjorie's marriage, they had gone driving together in Queenie's pony cart. An accident followed in which Marjorie suffered a broken collar-bone. Years later Queenie used to tell of my father's dreaded arrival from Windlestone and his description of the event to a repentant Charlie: 'Two damned silly women in a pony cart, reins under the horse's tail, the pony bolts, the cart overturns and my Marjorie's disfigured for life.' In the event, Marjorie soon mended, the storm blew over and all was serene again between Windlestone and Duncombe Park, the Feversham's home in Yorkshire.

Imagine, therefore, my excitement when one morning early in August a letter reached me from Charlie, telling me of his commission, that he wished to recruit a platoon in Durham County and asking me to help in this and perhaps later to command it, if I could pass the necessary tests and courses, military and physical. Within a few days, Charlie and Queenie motored over to Windlestone to see my mother who was one of my guardians. The formalities were soon completed and I was initiated into my first responsibilities, Marjorie telegraphing warm approval of the project as soon as she learnt of it.

The next week or two was spent in visiting as many potential recruits in County Durham as I could reach. For this I used my father's yellow Benz. Charlie had left me a list of possible volunteers which had been collected for him from many sources. My first venture was also one of the luckiest. Windlestone Grange was the farm nearest to us, even closer geographically than the home farm. Here I interviewed the farmer who admitted that a young man, John Grey, was 'champion with horses' and had thoughts of joining up. I soon met the quiet young Grey and his horses and I had no doubt that he would be a splendid asset to us, either in my platoon or with the battalion transport on whose behalf I was also looking out for suitable candidates. Naturally the farmer did not want to lose the young man but declared that he would not stand in his way if Grey's mind was made up. Grey said that it was, and so we gained a first-class volunteer for our transport.

It was sometimes tempting for riflemen in the line to refer to the transport section as a 'cushy' job. This was not a fair judgment. It is true that the men in the battalion transport did not have to spend days and nights in the line, or to go over the top in the literal sense, in a raid or an attack. On the other hand, night after night they had to bring up rations and supplies, sometimes in appalling conditions of mud and shelling, of delay and constant danger. To be shelled with horses and with mules was in some ways more unpleasant than to be shelled with men, for there was an added note of helplessness for the animals, and compassion and wretchedness when they were hit, and there was no flinging oneself flat on the ground for the man in transport.

Moreover, in an area of trench warfare, the artillery on either side would play at night upon the communications of the enemy. One battalion relieving another in the trenches

1. Lady Eden, a portrait by Sir Hubert von Herkomer

2. My sister Marjorie aged four

3. Myself aged three

4. My parents' Silver Wedding
and Jack's Coming of Age.
Left to right: Timothy, Marjorie,
my mother, Nicholas,
my father, myself.
My eldest brother, Jack,
is behind Nicholas

5. Eton 1910

10. Lady Grey

11. Myself aged fifteen

12 and 13. Sir William Eden, painting
Left, a portrait by
Prince Pierre Troubetskoy;
below, a photograph by
Prince Paul Troubetskoy, the sculptor

14 and 15. Water-
colours of
Windlestone by
Sir William Eden.
Above, the house
from the west;
right, Italian fountain
in the garden

16 and 17. Water-colours of Windlestone by Sir William Eden.
Top, the house from the east; *bottom*, above my father's writing table:
Degas' *Washerwomen*; on the right, Corot; on the left, Mark Fisher

18 (*top*). The new Napier car: my father, my mother,
Nicholas, myself, Marjorie

19 (*bottom*). Prince Francis of Teck and Lady Eden arriving for a bazaar
in aid of 6th Durham Light Infantry Volunteer Battalion, 1906

Grand Route de Péronne—   A.D. de ?

20 and 21. Drawings by
André Dunoyer de Segonzac from
Notes prises au front, 1917.
Left, *The Somme 1916*;
below, *Walking Wounded 1916*

erbois 19 16   A·S·

22 and 23. Aerial reconnaissance photographs of the Dammstrasse (Messines) before (22 March 1917) and after (8 June 1917) 9·2″ artillery bombardment

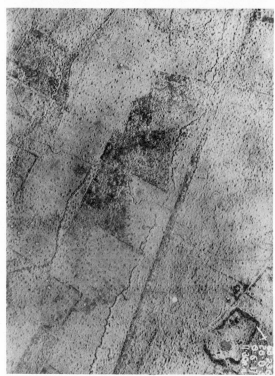

24. Myself aged eighteen
Aldershot, winter 1915

25. Myself aged twenty, with
Sgt Jim Dale (extreme
left) and 'Tiger' Pratt (extreme
right) Meteren, Flanders, 1917

might then be the target. More likely it would mean that the battalion transport coming up on their nightly duty, unenviable but also indispensable, were under shell-fire again. Grey, my first recruit, I am happy to say, came through the whole war unscathed, caring for his animals and sharing their dangers from Ploegstreet to the Somme, from Ypres to Messines, from the Menin Road to Italy and back again. For that was the road which the battalion was to travel. At the moment, however, we were only at our earliest stages.

A letter from Charlie told me that recruits were coming in well, including some from Durham County. These were not due to my efforts, but because word of the new battalion had got around.

Then my own tests began. The medical one was hardly more than a formality carried out by our family doctor, a well-read Irishman for whom my father had much affection. A strenuous course at an officers' school in the Eastern Counties was more formidable, and I was relieved when I got through it after a fashion and travelled north again to Helmsley, the market town which lay at the gates of Duncombe Park, where the battalion was by now assembled in fair strength.

This was my first introduction to my platoon and, though shy and acutely conscious of how little I knew, I enjoyed the experience immensely. After all these years one wonders why. I had no particular love for squad drill and spit and polish or any other of the ordeals of recruits, yet every day was full and satisfactory in its own way. Probably the answer was that we were all young, eager and knew that we were ignorant and were quite uninhibited about it.

This question of youth had much to do with it. I was not yet eighteen and a half, but several riflemen were younger and there had been some age-fudging, though we did not know it at the time. One well-built recruit, who could readily have passed for nineteen, was in fact then only sixteen and no doubt he was not alone. In my platoon only a small minority was over twenty-one, and none more than a year or two older.

This raised a formidable problem in the selection of

non-commissioned officers. Our parent regiment, the King's Royal Rifle Corps or Sixtieth Rifles, had in those days four regular battalions and two reserve battalions, which was twice the number of any other line regiment, except the Rifle Brigade. Even so, it was quite impossible to stretch their resources over a dozen or more active service battalions.

In the event our regular battalions were very generous to us in the supply of senior officers and N.C.O.s, but, with the best will in the world, that was all that they could do. The rest was our business and, after some deliberation among our seniors, it was decided that N.C.O.s should not be chosen by age and experience, because we could boast so little of either, but only by ability as best we could judge it over a short span. Incredible as it may seem, this worked out admirably. Admittedly it was a system of trial and error, but there were far fewer errors than one would imagine. In our company, and among the sergeants, there was not one.

A hastily recruited battalion such as this was essentially a parochial affair. Like my comrades, my interest was absorbed by my own platoon and I knew hardly anything of the world outside my company. Fortunately my company commander had given his first stripe to No. 9 Platoon's prospective sergeant before I arrived. Almost my height, but broader and stronger than I, with dark hair and blue eyes and a quick smile, Reg Park could have attracted many girls but was loyal to one. Equable and firm in temper, he took his duties very seriously, which was indeed the only way to do, since we expected to be in action against the enemy within six months. We knew nothing and there were few at hand to teach us.

With his friend Norman Carmichael, a fair-haired Northumbrian who occupied a like position in No. 10 Platoon and could both learn easily and express himself naturally in an attractive burr, Reg would spend long hours when off-duty studying manuals on tactics and military law, which they had bought out of their pay. Yet it would be wrong to give the impression of a collection of prim goody-goodies. Nothing of the sort, but we thought we knew what we were about, we were eager to get on with the job and we were, above all, young and full of life. We were not unhappy; there were drearier and darker times to come.

For myself, Helmsley was the first time in my life I had a job on my own to do and I enjoyed every moment of it. I was enthusiastic about my riflemen and they were tolerant of me, for they understood that we were all learning together. It was this sense of something which had to be shared that created a comradeship which was very strong and is not easy to describe. It links the survivors to this day in correspondence or at annual reunions, while our indefatigable honorary secretary keeps us posted about each other in a frequent newsletter. Maybe it was this comradeship which took the bite out of the most cheerless duties. Of course it may be said that it was the knowledge that we should soon be in action together with our lives at stake which forced a sense of unity. This played its part no doubt, but it would not be true to claim it as the whole explanation. There was something stronger and deeper, which I would call the finest form of friendship.

I soon found that I could rely upon Reg Park as a staunch and wise ally. He was two years older than I, which at that time of life can be quite an age in experience. Together we would discuss our platoon at length, which rifleman seemed to be coming on in his training, which had difficulties in drill or temperament and what we could do about either, or whether we could recommend riflemen for a stripe. Park took great pains over this analysis and over such material matters as the men's food. I was soon to learn that the riflemen understood all this effort and how much it meant to them.

Charlie Feversham was of middle-height, thick-set and with a moustache which today would be called bristling. The general effect could be intimidating, but he was a popular commanding officer with the riflemen, not least because he was essentially a countryman and so were many of them. He was not a professional soldier as was Foljambe, his second-in-command, but he had a good brain and enough experience to adapt himself to his new tasks as an infantryman. Despite which he was happiest on a horse and looked his best there.

Bob Iley, later to be my runner, said of his senior officers: 'We looked on Lord Feversham and Major Foljambe as detached country squires and both seemed to be rather over-awed by a Major H., a regular type who rode straight at you on his horse. We assumed that he represented the real Army and was there to knock us all into shape.'

*

In the early days of our training at Duncombe Park, Charlie thought it would be a good idea to exercise the whole battalion in open order, though we were still much under strength. To give a practical purpose to the enterprise, he decided that the battalion should deploy in the large park and drive the deer across it and through gates at its far side into another and wilder park. All went tolerably well at the start and the battalion advanced in fair order after their gentle foe, the mounted officers riding behind ús. At the last moment, however, the deer changed their minds; either they did not like the other park or they did not like us, but when almost within the gateways turned about sharply, leapt the extended line of astonished riflemen and galloped back swiftly into the park of their choice. Charlie was not very pleased, nor were we at our first defeat.

A visit by the general officer commanding Northern Command was another interlude in our routine. We sub-alterns were warned that the general was likely to cross-examine us on our knowledge of our riflemen and where they came from. I thought that this should hold no terrors for me. We were drawn up by companies in column of platoons. When the general reached No. 9, sure enough the question was put: 'And where do your men come from?' 'Durham, sir,' I replied. A nod, and then the same question to several riflemen as the front rank was inspected. Each man replied crisply and correctly, but as it naturally fell out that none of those questioned came from any town of any consequence known to the general, he was first puzzled, then exasperated. Finally, turning on me, 'I thought you said these men came from Durham,' he insisted. I hesitated, vaguely conscious that I must reply without suggesting limited knowledge of the geography of his command on the general's part.

Fortunately the colonel came to my rescue. 'These men are mostly from villages or quite small towns in the county, sir. Nearly all of them have some connection with the land, like Mr Eden's own family.' A grunt, a sigh of relief and the general moved off into Northumberland.

Meanwhile I had found myself in orders for a bombing course at Aldershot. My knowledge of bombs was limited to occasional accounts I had read of the activities of anarchists. More vividly I could recall grim illustrations in magazines of the exploding bomb among the guards and horses of the escort on King Alfonso's wedding drive. I did not really want to leave Helmsley and my platoon, but I was also curious when told that I was to be the only representative of the battalion on the course and that when I came back I should be expected to instruct others in the mysteries of this craft of which I knew nothing.

It soon emerged that not very much was known about it even at Aldershot at that stage of the war. Early in the proceedings we were told that we had to learn the power of explosives. To that end we were to witness a demonstration and we were shown a steel rail and a pound slab of T.N.T. The explosive with its detonator was placed under the rail and we were shepherded lower down the slope to watch the experiment. The fuse was lit and in a few seconds a convincing bang resulted. Then things began to happen. I was vaguely conscious of a cry close beside me, and of men falling and of an order to stay where we were by the officer in command. It was soon evident that some could not obey that order. Fragments of rail had been blown farther and harder than our instructors had anticipated and the casualties so far as I can recall were one dead and two or three wounded.

Inevitably there was an inquiry with some disciplinary consequences, but sad as this experience was, it taught me a lesson. Explosives are like dangerous living creatures, when handling them one can never, even for a second, relax one's guard.

Our bombs were then many of them primitive. The jam tin was still popular and we practised making it. The method was simple enough, once you knew how. Take any empty army ration jam tin and place on the bottom in the centre a priming charge of T.N.T., the size and shape of a small reel of cotton. Then fill the tin with any sharp stones or chips of flint available. Finally, insert a detonator with fuse attached into the hole in the reel of gun cotton. There remained the lighting of the fuse, which could be no easy task in pouring rain and conditions of trench warfare. A method advocated at that time was for a large match-head to be affixed to the fuse and for the bomber to tie an arm-band to his left arm with a strip of emery surface stitched to it. On this he was to strike the match-head attached to his fuse. Not surprisingly we found this more ingenious than practical.

Among the variety of bombs in which we were instructed was a recent type which instructors and pupils alike hailed as just the answer to our prayers. This was the Mills bomb which soon proved itself the best infantry bombing weapon of the war. I even seem to remember a lecture by its inventor Major Mills. We also learnt how to deal with unexploded examples of the German stick bomb, a useful weapon but inferior to our Mills because it did not fragment anything like as effectively.

While still on my bombing course I received a message that the battalion was moving to Aldershot and that I must await it there. I was sad at this, except that I knew that a spell at Aldershot or some military training area was inevitable before we could qualify for service overseas, therefore the sooner we got started the better. Even so, I found Aldershot depressing. The long lines of barracks interspersed with parade grounds succeeded each other in dreary rigidity. In the cold and rain of mid-winter the prospect was drab and dour.

We were in the Stanhope lines, solidly and drearily constructed in Victorian times to commemorate Wellington's victories. Barossa was our barracks and neither better nor worse than most. Material comforts were sadly reduced by war conditions. The rapidity with which divisions had succeeded each other in the same buildings, with the consequent damage and wear and tear, had left them battered and scarred. All this gave the Aldershot of those days a general atmosphere of something which had to be lived through, a stage between the eager recruit and the three-parts instructed, but not yet seasoned, soldier.

So began more than three months of intense training at the company, battalion, brigade and finally divisional level. I did not enjoy it, nor had I expected to. I suppose that we grew fitter and more familiar with our weapons as the weeks went by. But some of our activities were repetitious and others a waste of time. We seemed to concentrate too much on open warfare, the importance of which was continually being emphasized from above, whereas all we learnt from returned wounded and others showed that trench warfare was there to stay for quite a while.

It is true that in the last phase before we went to France we did spend a short spell, it may have been as much as forty-eight hours, in practice trenches on Laffan's plain, littered after the event with iron weights which were supposed to simulate ammunition. But there were so many highly polished boots walking about above ground, questioning and advising us on all manner of subjects, that the outcome for this sub-altern at least, was confusion rather than instruction. I consoled myself with the reflection that, once in real trenches overseas, we would at least be free to sort things out for ourselves.

How little we had learnt of trench warfare before we crossed the channel is illustrated by my memory of our second-in-command, Gerald Foljambe, the ablest soldier in the battalion, attempting to instruct riflemen how to set up an effective wire entanglement in a space between the support and reserve trenches, while we were actually in the line. Aldershot had taught us only a smattering of what we most needed to know.

*

In March 1916 Nicholas came home to Windlestone, already a hospital, for his final leave before going to sea and I was given a pass for forty-eight hours to join him for part of it. Though outwardly as gay and cheerful as ever, I had no doubt that Nicholas had found war-time Dartmouth hard going. Though he was without fear about the war or the enemy, I suspect he was not so confident about his immediate superiors in his new life.

As the two youngest, Nicholas and I were very close. It was impossible not to love the boy. In features if not in colouring he had some likeness to my father, in character he was most like Jack. Vital and venturesome and as a consequence often in trouble, no reproof or punishment could depress him for long, yet he had a gentle and affectionate nature. He was a favourite with all about Windlestone and I was devoted to him.

Our few hours together were flying fast when Nicholas questioned me as to when my pass ran out. I told him midnight Sunday. He asked when I had to be on parade; I replied Monday at 7.30 a.m., according to the orders when I left. Why then could I not take a later train, reach London around midnight and catch the milk train to Aldershot? I would be in plenty of time for the 7.30 parade.

I longed to say yes and to spend a few more hours with him, so that I hesitated, but something held me back. I told Nicholas that the colonel had been good to me in giving me this pass. We knew that we were soon going to France and leave was now hard to get. I just could not break my pass. Nicholas at once accepted this and we had our last talk together. For ever afterwards, Nicholas was a memory.

When I arrived back soon after midnight that Sunday evening, I found Guy Leatham, a friendly subaltern, waiting for me. 'Thank God you're back,' he said. 'You're in trouble for not turning up at the butts on Saturday. We parade at 6 a.m. and we feared you might risk the early morning train and be late. Then there would have been hell to pay.' I told Guy that the adjutant had given me leave earlier in the week: 'How could I then be in orders for the butts?' 'Well you were anyway,' he retorted. 'You ought to have found out the officer in charge and told him you had leave. He's not half mad at you, but the chief thing is that you're back. Better get some sleep.'

I had had a lucky escape. I had made the mistake of believing that leave granted at the top made repeated notifications lower down unnecessary, but such was the army. I was duly rebuked by the colonel and frowned upon by the musketry officer. Soon, however, we had more important things to think of as final preparations were made for overseas. It looked like France or Flanders, but we were told nothing definite.

Our transport officer was a personality. A former squadron sergeant-major of the Seventh Hussars, brought along with him by our colonel, he knew all that was to be known about horses, mules and waggons and not a little about humans. Everything about Potter was of generous proportions, including his weight, so that he was quite a problem to mount. However, a good strong beast was found and astride this Potter was to be seen in all weathers and all conditions at home and overseas, imperturbably doing more than his job so that the transport should not fail us. It never did.

Potter showed me much kindness. Though all subalterns unfamiliar with horses were put through a brief course in riding school, this was mainly to make sure that in an emergency, perhaps caused by casualties, any officer could ride if he had to. No officer below a company commander rated a mount for himself.

I was therefore delighted and flattered when one day after mess Potter asked me if I would like to exercise his horse. I made one or two trial attempts, closely watched by Potter, and was then allowed to take the horse out from time to time when his master was engaged on other sedentary duties, which he did not like but never skimped. All went well for a while until the time came for us to be vaccinated and inoculated for typhoid and tetanus. I was warned not to use my arm and was given an afternoon off. When, however, Potter's groom asked me if I would like to take the horse out, I just could not resist saying 'yes' especially since the horse, powerful animal as he was, had never pulled or given serious trouble of any kind.

As ill luck would have it I decided to go for a short canter on Laffan's plain where I met two other officers and never thought to tell them of my inoculation. We cantered off gently enough and then for some reason my horse began to pull. With my one arm I had a job to control him. The others, thinking I wanted to put on speed a little, stretched into a gallop and there we soon were, racing across Laffan's plain with my mount completely out of control.

It was all too long before I could pull up, the horse in a lather. I was so concerned about this and what Potter would think of my poor horsemanship that I hardly noticed my throbbing arm. I had no time to cool the animal down before I had to be back in our lines. Potter's Yorkshire groom looked unspoken reproaches and I had to tell him sketchily what had happened. Potter himself said never a word. Perhaps he thought, rightly, that I had learnt my lesson; but the doctor took it all badly and threatened to report me to the colonel for disobeying his warning, which would have been twice in a fortnight and might have had unhappy consequences for me. We had more than our full complement of officers and some were to be left behind with our reserve battalion when we sailed. As an early recruit I should have been disgraced to be one of these. Happily the doctor relented, probably with some help from my company commander, Captain Joe Pitt, who always stood by me.

The final panoply was on Laffan's plain with the whole division on parade. The King led the inspecting cavalcade, chatting to the generals as he rode down the line. Then came the march past the reviewing stand. We were left of the line, but did not disgrace ourselves despite the sudden change in tempo from the 'British Grenadiers' for the Royal Fusiliers who preceded us to our quick step and 'Lutzow's Wild Hunt'.

Guy and Marjorie had come to watch us. Guy was generous about the line we kept, but Marjorie thought that our division's physique compared badly with that of Guy's Canadian Brigade, who were also all volunteers. No doubt she was right, but this did not trouble us. It is strange now to reflect that our chief concern at the time was that we might arrive too late for the war. We did not; we had still more than two and a half years to go.

VII

'Plugstreet'

A few miles south of the Ypres Salient, but still just in Belgium, lay Ploegsteert Wood. If you were determined to make war, and trench warfare in particular, the wood in spring and summer provided the least disagreeable conditions for doing so. It was large enough for the front line to skirt its eastern edge, the support and reserve lines could be comfortably accommodated in its deeper recesses, while its western approaches were still sylvan and barely scarred by shell-fire at this stage of the war, in April 1916.

The trenches were well built and had strong points, communication trenches and support trenches, with dry dug-outs, and in the early morning the birds sang and the war seemed a long way off. One of the sergeants in our company wrote to his mother: 'This is what struck me as being very funny. You hear Whizz! – Bang! – Cuckoo! The birds sing all the time the shells are bursting – it is really astonishing. The nightingales sing when the machine-guns are firing during the night.'

Maybe some of these features made 'Plugstreet' wood seem a useful training ground for an unfledged division fresh from England. In any event, after some hard marching and counter-marching, presumably to deceive the enemy, along the *pavé* roads we were so to know so well, a party of officers and N.C.O.s was detailed for a spell in the trenches with the seasoned Scottish Division, then holding that section of the front. This was to be the first stage in our relief of the renowned Ninth Division.

The Germans, however, had other ideas and some useful intelligence reports. A night or two after our advanced details had begun to learn their way about, the enemy put down a short but intense bombardment of our forward areas followed by a raiding party, some of whom broke into our front line.

Fortunately the relief had not yet got under way, and the raiders were soon killed, wounded or repulsed by a company of these formidable Scottish troops whose departure they had been so eager to celebrate. A signboard left behind was just a shade premature. It read, 'Farewell Jocks. Welcome to the Forty-first division.'

This battle of the notice boards continued for most of the summer and we did not always get the best of it. One displayed from our lines triumphantly announced the capture of Lemberg by the Russians with many thousands of prisoners. A few days later came the tit for tat: 'England expects that France and Russia will do her duty.'

There followed some months of the routine of trench warfare: two weeks in the line, one in support and one in reserve and all in the wood. For newcomers this was not too monotonous and seemed to us worth while business compared with the parade ground at Aldershot. There were the defences to be strengthened, particularly the wire which had been much cut about in the shelling which preceded our take-over.

This was an eerie business but not as risky as it sounds. The ground was not so waterlogged as in the Ypres Salient nor were the trenches so close, sometimes as much as 150 to 200 yards apart. Our wiring parties soon picked up a few of the tricks of their trade, for instance that it was safer to stand stock still if an enemy Very light caught you by surprise rather than to drop flat on your face, when the movement might betray you.

No-man's-land was the unknown in our trench life. Visible in segments through a periscope by day but only effectively explorable at night, we could not be sure what was to be found there nor how far the enemy patrolled it. Our more experienced predecessors had told us what they could, but there was no real alternative to learning for ourselves, apart from the likelihood that the enemy had changed or would soon change his units also.

So began our frequent night patrols, exploring often on all

fours the shell-torn land, ditches, broken walls of buildings, even an occasional corner of what had once been some culti-vated plot. As the summer days lengthened the ground dried up and the grass began to grow, which had its advantage in concealment, though we would cut it ourselves in places where we wanted to improve our field of fire. With so many countrymen amongst us there were many jokes about hay-making. 'It will be in good fettle for leading tomorrow,' they would say.

As part of the process of trying to dominate no-man's-land, every rifleman was given his turn on patrol at some time. The terrain at night did not perplex these yeomen. Even so the first time, and particularly at the first scramble over the parapet, any man's body must feel pathetically conspicuous and naked. After a while one learnt that there was little real danger unless familiarity led to carelessness about noise. Then a burst of machine-gun fire, even if not well aimed, could teach a salutary lesson. So our activities in no-man's-land became a war within a war and, for me at least, the more meaningful part of it.

The ordered trenches at Plugstreet soon gained familiarity, like some hamlet at home that one knew well. This applied also to no-man's-land. As a result of several night patrols over the same ground, I thought I could find my way through the darkness. The ruins of a house lay just beyond the front line on our right. One night returning with my patrol I came upon something growing in the pervading shambles, neither nettle nor weed, a flower in full bloom from this shattered home. Eagerly I picked it and bore it off to our small, ill-ventilated dug-out, with happy thoughts of pressing it and sending it home to Windlestone.

After stand-down, I returned to the dug-out with Joe Pitt, who exclaimed as he entered: 'What is the filthy stink in here?' My poor discovery was an onion in flower.

We had already begun to suffer the inevitable trickle of casualties. I loathed each one of them. For more than six months now we had worked and trained together in our small group, No. 9 Platoon. I had grown to know my rifle-men and to like them immensely. I tried to put out of my mind the inevitable and bloody side to our business, perhaps with the result that I felt each casualty the more.

An early incident of this kind forced reality upon me. At this period of the war and probably throughout, shrapnel caused more casualties than high explosive, and the enemy would occasionally treat us to an unwelcome salvo at some point over our sector. On this particular sunny morning he burst a few well-aimed shells low over my platoon's front line.

At first I was relieved to find that our only casualty appeared to be a slight flesh wound in the shoulder for young Spencer, what most of us would have regarded as the perfect 'Blighty'.

Spencer was typical of these yeoman volunteers. Of medium height, slight in build, but physically stronger than he seemed, he was a quiet, keen but unassertive boy and a general favourite. Reg Park and I had been discussing only a day or two before whether we should recommend him for a stripe.

I can see the setting a few minutes after Spencer's wound as clearly as if it were yesterday. The sunshine, Spencer with his tunic off his right shoulder, the slight wound in the white flesh being bandaged by our stretcher-bearer over its coating of iodine. Spencer was sitting on the fire-step and smiling gently at the mingled questions and good wishes we offered while his successor already stood in his place watching the disinterested enemy lines. My own feeling was one of relief that for some months at least he would be out of it.

Later that morning, when I was back at battalion headquarters on some bombing officer duty, I asked our doctor about Spencer, eagerly suggesting that he would be at home for quite a while and that I should try to get him to hospital at Windlestone. The doctor's quiet reply shook me: 'I hope so, Boy, but remember that shrapnel wounds are always dangerous.' It seemed to me though that this warning must be professional caution, so that I was unprepared when, a few days later, a message came through that Spencer had died of his wound in hospital. This was our first sharp contact with sudden death and we were utterly miserable. The passage of years has never blunted it. We had yet to learn that it was the chance deaths in the trenches which left a sharper imprint than the wholesale slaughter of a battle.

It was, I think, my company commander who first dubbed me 'the Boy', though the riflemen later claimed that they had, and it is true that when I was commissioned I was by several years the youngest of the company's subalterns. However, even when that condition was only relative the name still stuck, at least until the heavy casualties of the Somme made a nonsense of it and left me with only a memory of most of those who had used it.

Our new doctor was our gift from the gods. He was everything that a battalion could ask of its medical officer and much more besides, and there was no reason why he should have come our way, except that he was determined to serve with a combatant unit. A young Canadian and a qualified surgeon at a hospital in Toronto, Hart's skills were in a sense wasted upon us, and he was at length winkled out to the advantage of a base hospital, but not for over a year during which much was to befall him and us and many riflemen were to owe him their lives.

*

Perhaps it was increased artillery activity further south or expectation of an Allied attack at some point, or even our own increased patrol activity, which made the enemy jumpy. Whatever the cause, our front livened up as summer advanced. On one occasion we suffered unusually heavy shelling around the dangerous hour before dawn. It seemed to us that a raid might be imminent, so we countered with some lively rifle and machine-gun fire on the forward areas opposite. The shelling grew heavier, so did our firing but no attack developed. We never knew whether any was intended.

Inevitably our front line and the communication trench were badly battered in these exchanges. We had also suffered casualties. Only one of these was fatal and we could do nothing effective, though we tried all we knew. The wound was in the jugular and we could not even check the bleeding. It was horrible to be so helpless. I asked Hart later about it and he told me that even if he had been on the spot it was unlikely that he could have saved the unfortunate man's life, which was only relative comfort.

An hour or two later while we were still sandbagging and repairing the gaps in our defences, the colonel came round, spoke to some of the riflemen and, as he left, turned to me: 'You haven't shaved this morning, Anthony, nor have the men of your platoon.' 'No, sir, not yet; it's been a pretty rough night.' He nodded: 'I know, but you should all be shaved by nine. See to it next time.' I was rather dunched, but he was right.

Two hours on and four hours off was the way the watch went in the line and matters were so arranged that no platoon commander and his sergeant were on watch together. As a result I grew to know the other platoon sergeants in the company really well. At night, especially if things were quiet, there were hours when we had to be wakeful with idle time to while away. That is how Norman Carmichael and I became friends, which we have been ever since. We did not lack opinions and we aired them freely on any subject that came up.

Norman had an active mind with a quite exceptional gift for clear and incisive expression. He was not a man you could fool and it was therefore no surprise when, after being wounded in the Somme campaign, he was commissioned to serve the 'tanks' which at this time we had not even heard of.

We talked of the war without any clear view of its duration. We expected a new Allied offensive at some time, but having heard the Ninth Division speak of Loos when we relieved them, we just did not know what to make of its chances. We spoke of after the war too and were naïve about the future, but I think not alone in our optimism.

Norman was convinced that we should be a more united country after the war. We had all been so much mixed up together in a battalion like ours and in so many others of which we knew, that it was hardly conceivable the nation should be divided again as it had been. Perhaps if more men like Norman and others with his point of view had survived, the outcome might have been happier. We had neither of us a glimpse of the casualties still to come, still less of the difference in outlook and experience which was to grow between many at home and the volunteers overseas. Meanwhile these talks on still summer nights in Plugstreet wood cleared my mind. Many of the ideas which I hold to this day stemmed from them, particularly a sense of the irrelevance and unreality of class distinction.

*

The bane of our life was working parties, usually at night. For these unwelcome chores men had to be constantly provided. The worst assignment that summer was to carry gas cylinders up communication trenches and to install them in our front line. This took many weary and exhausting hours. The most disagreeable part of the business was that we had to wear gas masks rolled up on the top of our heads under our tin hats all the time. These masks, effective only against chlorine, were damp and impregnated with some unpleasant-smelling stuff which, as we were soon to learn, could bring out an ugly and itching rash on the forehead. The masks had to be at the ready in this way for fear that a chance shell or even machine-gun fire might puncture a cylinder, which did not add to the attractions of the whole exercise. Then it rained and the slippery duckboards, slithering cylinders, traversed trenches, stinking masks and stumbling, swearing men, added up to a long black night in C Company's memory.

Whether the gas did the enemy any harm we never learnt. Certainly their gas alarms went off with a crescendo of warning which seemed to spread north and south, from the sea to the Swiss frontier.

Some few weeks earlier we had been alerted by a gas alarm which was the signal for our escape from a grave danger, though only our seniors knew of it at the time. The Germans were attempting an attack with a new gas. Happily for us, either due to freakish weather or because the gas had been insufficiently weighted, it soared above our lines and only came down in some fields a mile or two in our rear, killing some unfortunate cows.

Bob Iley had been my 'runner', or bearer of messages to and from company headquarters, since early days. We soon discovered that he had an excellent bump of locality, a gift which he developed until he had an uncanny facility for finding his way around or across a battered maze of trenches at any time or anywhere. He could read the gunfire and make a dash for it between salvoes. In the days before walkie-talkies, with uncertain field telephones, runners were a lubricating element of the First World War; unless they got through, nothing went right. I could not be surprised, therefore, though I was selfishly sorry, when battalion head-quarters ordered Iley to report for duty there. A few months later I had every reason to be grateful for this wise selection.

*

One lovely afternoon towards the end of June, when we were in the support line, Bob sought me out and told me that the colonel was at company headquarters and wanted to see me there at once. Off I went, somewhat puzzled as to what this summons could be about. I found Charlie Feversham alone outside our company headquarters' dug-out, looking glum. 'I want a word with you, Anthony,' he said, and led the way into the bay of a neighbouring unoccupied trench.

A quiet lull in the wood, a brilliant summer's day and Charlie standing there disturbed and unhappy. There had been a big naval engagement with the German fleet in the North Sea, he said. While he did not know the outcome in any detail, it was already certain that our battle cruiser squadron had lost heavily. Among others, Nicholas's ship, the *Indefatigable*, had gone down. I asked about survivors and was told there could be very, very few, if any. It appeared that the *Indefatigable* had been blown up and had sunk im-mediately.

In my wretchedness I could hardly believe it. Nicholas and I had so often talked of possible naval action. Though I knew little enough about it, I had an inbred faith in the absolute superiority of the Royal Navy. I had had no definite opinion as to whether the German navy would come out. I was sceptical about it, but I was deeply convinced that if it did, the Royal Navy would be more than a match for it.

I suppose it was my unquestioning confidence which had

stopped me from ever weighing up the possible cost in casualties of a naval battle. Of course I knew that Nicholas ran some risks, but I had never doubted for a moment that he would come through all right, whatever happened to the rest of us.

More than four years separated me from my elder brother Timothy, and no less than nine from Jack and ten from Marjorie. Nicholas and I were not three years apart. For as long as I could remember we had shared everything, nannies, governesses, tutors, ponies. Despite the occasional and inevitable squalls, we preferred each other's company to any other in the world. Nicholas was cheerful by nature and fun to be with. Quick-moving and impetuous, he was not conspicuously clever at his books, unless for some reason they appealed to him. He was too impatient for the more tedious lessons which often came our way, but any outdoor activity attracted him, especially if it had to do with animals. A mongoose, a jerboa, and, of course, several ferrets had formed part of his constant menagerie. At the Battle of Jutland he was just sixteen. It was considered in those days a suitable age for a midshipman, not only to go into battle, but to be in command of able seamen. In charge of his gun-turret at the Battle of Jutland, Nicholas had no chance to prove his worth.

*

It was fortunate for me that during these weeks I was heavily occupied with my two sets of duties as platoon commander and as battalion bombing officer, or perhaps thoughtful seniors had arranged it that way. I was over-worked, with no time to think.

Our bombing activities were concentrated in a small dug-out near battalion headquarters. There I had my bombing squad of a corporal and three or four riflemen. We had a variety of duties, the most important of which was to inspect the supplies of bombs in the charge of companies, to make sure they were kept greased and in good condition and the detonators cared for. I never lost my sense of careful respect for these last touchy explosives, which was no doubt just as well for my survival.

We manufactured a few old-fashioned 'jam-tins' and a few sulphur bombs which could be thrown at any time when we wanted to test the wind. We had also to keep up our knowledge of our own types of bombs and rifle grenades and those of the enemy so that we could advise or deal with either as the need arose, as it did from time to time. Finally, there was my senior, in the shape of the brigade bombing officer, to be reported to and satisfied. It was a full programme, but on the whole I enjoyed it, principally because I was on my own in working at it. Bombs were not universally popular.

Plugstreet was not as ill-sited for observation of the enemy as the Ypres Salient. The terrain was just flat, not sloped against us, but the difficulty of any observation of the enemy lines remained. In all secrecy an intelligent helper in need was devised, though we had no more to do with this than to provide the experts with some muscular help. As our line at Plugstreet ran along the forward edge of the wood, it was studded at intervals with broken and splintered trees. It was decided that on a moonless night one of these wounded victims of war should be dug up and replaced by an exact replica in steel, hollow so that an observer could climb up inside to view an extensive sector of the enemy's forward trenches.

As the tree chosen was in our front line and little more than a hundred yards from the enemy, the outcome of the operation depended on the silence and speed with which it could be completed. The sappers had done their job well, so had the camouflage experts and the new observer was safely mounted unperceived. Our feelings about our unexpected recruit were mixed. His value was evident, if he could remain undiscovered, but if a chance shell should expose the steel tree we must expect a violent bombardment to destroy it. Fortunately no such mischance befell while we were in the wood.

Our one week out of four in reserve was a strange hybrid life. We lived in 'Hunter's Avenue', a series of unimpressive forts offering no protection from shell fire. As they were far back in the wood, however, the trees sheltered us to some extent, while the general sense of peace and greenery and the change from trench life and duties were welcome. The random shell did not seem significant.

Rats were a plague in the trenches. The Plugstreet specimens were modest and mouse-like compared with the larger and fiercer ones we were to meet later at Ypres. Even so, this being our first experience of these vermin at close quarters, they were much resented, not least by Reg Park for their greed after rations and the added dirt and discomfort they created for his men.

Soon after we had taken over in Hunter's Avenue, Reg reported to me in disgust that the rats were as bad as in the line; he would like to go after them. I wished him luck. An hour or so later two or three shells came over, one of them as it seemed to me uncomfortably close. I came out of my fort to find out if any damage had been done and saw a rifleman coming down the duckboards at the double towards me. There had been a direct hit on one of the forts and Sergeant Park had been killed.

I went back with the rifleman. A 5·9 shell had devastated the fort and Reg had been killed instantly. Later we reconstructed the short sad story. Reg had chosen this unused fort in which to set up his rat-traps. He had one rifleman to help him and had just sent him out to get some more wire when the shell came. Thus poor Reg had fulfilled the front-line soldier's philosophy that if somewhere there was a shell with your name on it, it would find you out wherever you were.

We buried him in a little cemetery behind the wood and I lost a friend I have never forgotten. I also learnt how much the sergeant had meant to the men of his platoon, something I had not been experienced enough to understand before.

One of an officer's less welcome tasks was to censor his men's letters home. That week every letter contained a reference to Park's death, which was natural enough. More extraordinary was the warmth and, more particularly, the understanding of the extent to which their sergeant had spent himself on their behalf. This was most vehemently expressed by the greediest man amongst them who wrote: 'We have lost our sergeant. He was a good man and watched out for our interest. Now I suppose the officers will take more of our rations.' How much Reg would have laughed at that.

⁂ VIII ⁂

The Raid

We could hardly hope to find Park's equal from our own resources and fortunately we did not have to try. His successor was an experienced regular soldier fully trained on active service. Quick, responsible and firmly knowledgeable in all he had to do, Bert Harrop was the best type of Greenjacket non-commissioned officer. A Yorkshireman, whose home was in Sheffield, he was soon accepted with respect by No. 9 Platoon. He did us all a power of good.

The opening stages of the Battle of the Somme made themselves felt even in our tranquil sector. One afternoon in the line I was on duty at company headquarters when Major Foljambe called in. Though I knew him little at this time, he had already impressed me more than any of our senior officers. Perhaps this was because he was so quietly professional. Always impeccably turned out, he was the reverse of the orthodox. For instance, none of the repeated ordinances of those days would induce him to grow a moustache. What pretexts he professed I do not know, but Foljambe was always clean-shaven. Perhaps it was his charm that did it. I never knew a man who had more and this readily compensated for his bursts of temper, occasionally directed at human frailty, but more frequently at the military machine.

Foljambe was too intelligent to tolerate officialdom in its cruder forms, nor would he acquiesce without protest in decisions he considered ill-judged. Maybe he would have held higher commands had he been less outspoken, but that, I am sure, never troubled him for an instant. As Eddie Worsley, his successor as second-in-command, was to say many years later: 'You know, Anthony, the riflemen would do anything for Foljambe. They knew he would never let them down.'

That afternoon Foljambe said to me: 'I want to talk to you about the enemy front line opposite this sector. You know this piece of no-man's-land pretty well, and I understand you have reported on a sentry who appears to patrol opposite here. Can you tell me anything more about this?' I explained that I had once heard what sounded like a sentry on patrol in the trench, and so had Sergeant Harrop on another occasion, but the sentry was by no means always there. Sometimes we could hear men talking and sometimes all would be quiet.

Foljambe then told me that divisional headquarters was anxious to get an identification of the Germans opposite, who it was suspected had only recently taken over. For this purpose a number of raids were to be attempted at night. He thought that our sector offered probably the best chance of success. A raid by a section of my platoon would be staged first. I was to discuss the details with him and with Captain Pitt. I was to bring Sergeant Harrop along with me, but neither he nor I was to tell anybody else about it.

Our plans were carefully laid. No-man's-land at this point was eighty to a hundred yards wide. I was to command the raiding party which was to be small. With three riflemen who knew the ground well, we would form the main body. Harrop with two more riflemen would take up a chosen position in no-man's-land on our right and about half-way across. From there he could support us if we needed it when in the German trench, or cover our withdrawal. If necessary he could also create a diversion which might confuse the enemy.

There was to be no artillery preparation. The essence was to be secrecy and surprise on a night with little moon. Two riflemen with an uncanny aptitude for night patrol, Arthur Pratt, known to us as 'Tiger', who happily survived the war, and Tom Liddell, who would brave any danger and was killed within a week of the armistice, were chosen for the toughest job. They were each to cut a gap through the German wire. The third rifleman, who was a skilled bomber, and I would be with them, and the wire once cut, we would jump into the German trench and kill or capture the sentry. At the least we should get some identification mark.

The odds did not seem all that heavy against us. By this time we had established supremacy in no-man's-land. The enemy hardly ever showed himself and as a result had not even cut the long grass close to his wire. He had therefore no field of fire and we had once or twice patrolled close to the German wire without being spotted.

All the same, I had my worries. Though I was given some latitude in the time I took, I knew that I was expected back at the latest an hour before dawn, so that the raid planned by the company on our left, against our possible failure, could be launched. More serious was the spasmodic, but still above average, enemy artillery fire for two nights before our raid. It was not that I thought this would affect our own plans or action, for it was mostly directed at the support or reserve lines, or even farther back. My anxiety was simply that this activity might alert our opposite numbers in the German front line, and if we were to have any chance of success we must have a normally quiet night.

Finally I had one further problem. We had worked out our line of retreat. Almost at right-angles between the two opposing lines ran an old field ditch, deeper at our end than at the enemy's. This could be our salvation, on the other hand, the Germans might know of it. I agreed that if need be we should make for it, but nobody was to enter it unless I signalled that they could do so.

The first moves went according to plan. We worked our way across no-man's-land without incident, and Pratt and Liddell began to cut the enemy wire. This was tough and rather thicker in its long grass than we had reckoned. Even so we made good progress and there were only a few strands left to cut, so that we were right under the German trench, when suddenly, jabber, jabber, and without warning two German heads appeared above the parapet and began pointing into the long grass. We lay flat and still for our lives, expecting every second a blast of machine-gun fire or a bomb in our midst. But nothing happened. After a little more jabber, the heads disappeared and all was quiet again.

We lay without moving for what must have been nearly an hour. There were no abnormal noises from the German line nor was the sentry on patrol. Less than four minutes of wire-cutting would complete our task and I had to decide what to do next. I touched Pratt and Liddell to go on.

The job was just about done when all hell seemed to break loose right in our faces. The German trench leapt into life, rifles and machine-guns blazed, Very lights soared up and the place seemed to us as light as day. Incredibly none of this bombardment touched us, presumably because we were much closer to the German trench, within their wire and only a foot or two from the parapet, than the enemy imagined possible. As a result the firing was all aimed above and beyond us, into no-man's-land or at our own front line.

Once more we had dropped down into the long grass and made no move until the firing eased and the Very lights dimmed a little. Then I signed to my small section to begin to crawl back. Our first blow was the old field ditch, a German machine-gun sputtered down it at intervals, so there was no choice but a slow creep back across the open, praying that no Very light would expose us too clearly. All went well for a while, and we were about fifty yards from our front line when I heard what seemed a groan at my left hand. Signalling to the others to go on I moved a few yards to investigate. There I found Harrop lying in the lip of a shallow shell-hole bleeding profusely from a bad bullet wound in his thigh and two riflemen trying to help him.

Harrop was weak from loss of blood, but still calm and decided. As we fixed a tourniquet on his leg he kept insisting, 'Tighter, tighter, or I'll bleed to death.' If he was to have any chance, we must get him back into our line without delay. The question was, how. The firing was now sporadic rather than intense, but as I crouched beside Harrop I knew we must have a stretcher if we were to get him in before dawn. I said so and one of the two young riflemen with Harrop, Eddie Bousefield, at once volunteered to go.

In a few minutes he was back in our line, had collected a

stretcher and a fellow rifleman, and rejoined us without being spotted. Then came the difficult decision. We had only fifty yards to go, and even though we stooped, we would all four have to stand up to carry Harrop's stretcher. The longer we waited the better the chance of the night growing quieter, but the worse for Harrop and the more extended the risk for us all. I wanted to get it over with, and we did. To this day I do not know whether the enemy saw the stretcher and held his fire, or saw nothing in the flickering Very lights. There was a chilly feeling down our spines anyway.

Harrop suffered much pain, two years in hospital and thirty-three operations, but he recovered and we met from time to time. On my writing table is a small and very pretty gold pen-knife from his native Sheffield. It is always there.

*

'Tiger' Pratt was the mildest and gentlest of men. Short of stature, with an open expression, a disarming smile and perfect manners, at a first meeting he would probably be written down as a natural salesman, which was precisely what he had been. During our first spell in the front line we soon learned that there was another Pratt. An immediate volunteer for no-man's-land he was a 'tiger' for patrols, stealthy and determined. He appeared to see like a cat in the dark and was as blood-thirsty a night prowler in those fetid landscapes as one could hope to find. It was impossible not to respect and like him, and his fellow-riflemen made no mistake at his christening.

If at the time when I left my platoon to become adjutant I had been asked who was my best fighting rifleman I would have said Tom Liddell, and that was only after three or four months of trench warfare. He never changed up to the day he was killed serving with another battalion of our regiment a few days before the armistice, after two and a half years of truly active service. Recommended on separate occasions, while with the Yeoman Rifles, for both a Distinguished Conduct Medal and a Military Medal he was awarded the latter, though he richly deserved both. Tom never sought promotion or reward and I do not believe that either interested him; it was just that the more tense and dangerous a situation, the more his courage rose to meet it. When in an exceptionally bloody offensive at the end of September 1917, his company had lost all its officers and senior N.C.O.s, Tom, then a junior sergeant, took over command as if this was the most natural event in the world, rallied his riflemen and led them to their objective which they consolidated and held.

Liddell's other gift was a high technical efficiency in whatever he undertook. So it was that, besides being a good shot and skilled in the use of our variety of bombs and grenades, we had not been in Plugstreet many weeks before he was our swiftest operator in strengthening our barbed wire and cutting through the enemy's. We did not ask for volunteers for a raiding party, the company or platoon commander would detail the men but, almost inevitably, 'Tiger' and Tom chose themselves.

*

A few weeks after our abortive raid I found myself temporarily cast in a new role, that of battalion billeting officer. In this capacity I travelled by railway truck in the company of a heavy army bicycle to Pont Rémy on the Somme. There my bicycle and I got off and I pedalled my way in brilliant summer weather to the village of Françières. Here our battalion was to rest and train for several weeks. Official information did not go beyond this, nor were we at all troubled at what might follow.

My billeting duties were not heavy. I had been given a list of the billets available to us by the French authorities at Pont Rémy. Now, with the village gendarme, I was to make a tour of them, meeting such local worthies as were not out in the fields and allot the accommodation between companies, an invidious exercise which was likely to earn me some criticism when the battalion arrived. Meanwhile I enjoyed myself.

We began our tour at the Château of Monsieur le Comte, a simple but pleasing seventeenth-century house, austerely bounded by high iron palings, where our colonel was allocated a wing for himself and his headquarters. My memory is of a courteous host and that all was to go well between the two 'Messieurs les Comtes', St Pol and Feversham. There was nothing to complain about in our billets, the village was all smiles and I spent a pleasant interlude in the inn with an omelette and a bottle of wine, before the time came to trundle my bicycle back again to meet the battalion at Pont Rémy and show the advance party to their quarters.

The heat, the dusty lanes, the smell of the fields, the quiet of Françières apart from farm-house noises, all made the sharpest contrast with the trenches we had left. So many of my summer holidays since childhood had been spent in France that it was like being drawn back into a past which I had known and loved.

Our training was strenuous, the weather was glorious and we became very fit. Looking back upon those days, I suppose that I was never again to see a battalion so primed in all respects during more than two years of war which were to follow. While we knew that the field exercises we were put through must lead to some action somewhere, we knew nothing more and it is fair to say that our mood was eager rather than apprehensive.

There were occasions when we had to advance in line through a wood, eventually debouching from it, and our night operations had the same character. At the time I was more impressed by an enthusiastic company commander who carried his realism so far as to start in the middle of the night picking up, sparks flying, the château drive, to form a defensive trench covering his newly captured position. His activities were soon smothered and remedied, but none of this seems to have given any of us younger ones an inkling that the wood in which we were manoeuvring was the prototype of Delville Wood, already known as one of the bloodiest battlegrounds of the Somme fighting.

Maybe we were not curious or, more likely, we were working too hard and were too physically stretched to think much beyond what the next day or two might bring.

My clearest memory is of the company marching back to billets along a dusty country road, tired but cheerful and singing, so that even Norman Carmichael's firm repetition of the step to No. 10 Platoon could scarcely be heard. The next night, just before the light of dawn, the Yeoman Rifles wound up the hill out of Françières to entrain for the Somme. As they sang 'There's a long, long trail a-winding', they were at the peak of their strength and pride.

*

These early days of September continued unbroken, but they had brought the billeting officer some new orders. I was to entrain once more at Pont Rémy, this time in the opposite direction for a small station near Albert on the Somme, where I was to meet a representative of our brigade headquarters who would indicate our camping area to me. This was a simple enough business; the bare slope of a hillside was to be our site until further orders.

Those few miles from Pont Rémy had wrought a transformation. We were on the edge of the battle area and I began to see real devastation. The sound of the guns was continuous and as night fell their flashes lit up the sky in a great arc from north to south of us. The town of Albert lay below us with the dislodged statue of the Virgin still precariously suspended from her church roof. All around us were the sights and sounds of war as I had never known it. Bivouacs everywhere, the roads choked with transport, troops, guns and ambulances. I was awed, but also not a little thrilled. In a local shop postcards of 'the Basilica after several bombardments' were on sale.

When I met the battalion the next day and told our colonel of our bare field he did not seem greatly interested, but stood for a moment outside his truck, *40 hommes 8 chevaux* listening to the guns and drinking in the scene, as strange to him as to me. Then he turned to Foljambe and said with deep feeling, 'The real thing at last, thank goodness.'

❖❖ IX ❖❖

Battle of the Somme

The following afternoon our company commander sent for me and told me that new orders had just come down from division limiting the number of officers and N.C.O.s we were to take into action. As a consequence, each company had to leave behind two officers and two senior sergeants as well as a percentage of junior N.C.O.s. In our last weeks at Plugstreet and since, one or two junior officers had joined us and I imagined that these would be left out of the battle. So I asked casually who was to stay behind. He said, 'You, Boy,' and mentioned another comparatively senior officer. I was outraged and exclaimed that he could not possibly leave me behind. I had been with the battalion since its early days, I had helped recruit my platoon, I could not desert them in their first major action.

Joe Pitt said that he knew this would be my reaction, but the decision was not his. Which officers to take and which to leave behind had been a carefully considered decision of the colonel's in conclave with Foljambe and the adjutant. I was not to be appeased and asked to see the colonel. This was granted and I reported to him that evening.

He heard me out patiently. I told him that I was sure he would understand my feelings. I had spent the whole of the past year in preparation for this, I could never look my men in the face again if I failed them now. Charlie Feversham shook his head: 'It's not like that, Anthony. I shall speak to the battalion before we move off and explain this among other things. Of course Joe Pitt would like to have you with him. Don't you think I would like to have Foljambe with me? But it cannot be. We have to take some thought for the battalion's future.' Then with a smile he added: 'Don't take it so hard, there will be plenty more battles for you before this business is through,' and dismissed me.

I was still not comforted. Amongst other things it seemed unfair that young officers who had less experience than I should lead men into battle in my place. There was one for whom I was particularly troubled. His father was a missionary in China and he had spent much of his life there until at eighteen he volunteered to come home to fight. Slight but well built, young Harman played all games well and was popular with the riflemen. They would follow him anywhere, but I also knew that he was utterly fearless. He would not throw his life away, because he was a religious boy, but he would not take the slightest precaution, and I was anxious for him. He was killed later leading his company and his name is on the Menin Gate at Ypres.

A day or two before these events, our adjutant received orders to send an officer and two N.C.O.s to witness an exercise to be carried out by armoured vehicles. The receipt of this summons aroused no particular interest and some imagined that tanks, as the new machines were called, were an improved form of water container. This would have been welcome, since our water supply on the Somme came up in old petrol tins, and even our tea reeked of the stuff. When our envoys returned from the demonstration, however, they had a fantastic tale to tell. The creatures they had seen were strongly armoured and said to be impervious to rifle or machine-gun fire and only vulnerable to a direct hit by a 5·9 shell. They had caterpillar tracks for wheels and had surmounted a trench with ease and crushed in a dug-out. They could even knock down a small tree and their pace would enable them to accompany infantry in their advance in battle. This they intended to do on our next zero day.

The secret had been well kept, and the excitement and questioning was all the more intense. There were sceptics, of course, but these were subdued when, on the move to their assembly positions two days later, all ranks of the battalion saw the monsters for themselves. Better still, in the path of one of them stood a broken-down old machine-gun hand-cart, apparently left behind as unserviceable by some earlier unit. This was a heavy vehicle to handle and unpopular. Without deviating a hair's breadth, the tank crunched on over the stranded cart and splintered it to matchwood. A spontaneous cheer from the expectant riflemen made everyone feel better.

*

That day in camp, September 14th, I could think of nothing except the battalion on its approach march, so when in the early afternoon the post arrived from England, I at once asked leave to ride up with it. It was not thought I could get further than battalion headquarters and back before nightfall. My slow progress soon justified this forecast. Whole villages were reduced to mounds of rubble, red with brick dust, identified only by their names on a giant board. The roads were chock-a-block with transport of every description, troops, guns, supplies, Red Cross ambulances.

Eventually I found our battalion headquarters in an assembly trench at the back of Delville Wood and handed over my small bundle of letters from home. They were very welcome, but I was less so. 'Get along back as soon as you can,' ordered the colonel, adding not unkindly: 'You know that you have no real business here.'

Reports of the battle which reached us about noon the next day were that the battalion had made a good advance against the Bavarian division which faced them, that this was continuing, led by the colonel and the adjutant; there had been numerous casualties. In the early evening came an order from brigade headquarters, the colonel had been killed and the adjutant seriously wounded, Major Foljambe was to go up and take over command of the battalion, which was to be relieved during the night. At daylight Foljambe returned to camp with two officers and sadly depleted other ranks, all that was left of the battalion.

We later pieced together what had happened as best we could. Two battalions of 124th Infantry Brigade, our own and Tenth Queen's, were by the afternoon of September 15th in line on a position east of Flers and facing the Gird ridge. They appeared to be well in advance of the troops on either flank, but capable of holding the ground they had taken. At this juncture the brigade commander, Clemson, and the commanding officer of the Queen's, Oakley, a perceptive and experienced regular soldier, were together with Feversham and discussing an order which had just come through, presumably from division, instructing both battalions to attack and capture the 'next objective'. This was the Gird ridge, a formidable obstacle where the enemy was strongly entrenched with his wire uncut and his defences intact.

Oakley surmised that the order was based on a mistaken belief that the brigade was still on its earlier objective, and he may have been right. In any event the order as it reached them was deplorably vague. The brigadier, however, decided that it must be carried out as received, apparently considering that a further advance might bring help to the divisions on our right which were held up around Les Boeufs and Morval and had suffered heavy casualties.

The attack took place without further preparation and failed with heavy loss. Feversham was killed leading his riflemen and Honey, his adjutant, lost an eye. Oakley was wounded and his adjutant killed. There was soon no senior officer left in either battalion, and it says much for the sub-alterns that they were able to rally their units and dig in for the night without losing much ground. The Gird ridge was not captured for several weeks and only then after more hard fighting. It may be that from corps headquarters the depth of the Forty-first Division's advance raised hopes of a break-through, but the Gird ridge defences were much too strong for that without effective preliminary artillery bombard-ment. The methods of Messines 1917 had not yet been learnt on the Somme in 1916.

On the afternoon of September 16th came the roll-call, and my saddest hour with C Company. It would not have been so bad if we had not known each other so well, but after anything up to a year of living and training together, we were friends. It fell to me to call the roll. After each silence, and there were so many, I had to ask who had last seen Ser-geant Carmichael or Rifleman Hunter, or whoever it might be, and enter what scraps of information we could gather.

As we finished I noticed Foljambe standing a few yards away and silently watching the scene. He beckoned me to him and said quietly, 'Eden, you'll be adjutant.' I was amazed, excited, above all scared. 'But, sir,' I managed to protest, 'I know nothing about it.' 'Never said you did,' came the curt reply. 'Report to the orderly room at five o'clock.'

In the interval I escaped to the casualty clearing station. The scene I found is dim now, the crowded tents, the operating theatre at one end, the tired surgeons, the bandaged figures, most of them silent on their stretchers and still in their torn and muddied uniforms; but none of this overawed me, for I found several of my riflemen and gleaned news of others.

One conversation I remember. We will call its principal Rifleman R. Quick, bright and a good footballer, Reg Park and I early decided that R. was a possible candidate for a stripe. After some patient watching we persuaded our company commander to give him one, but we had reckoned without R.'s capacity for getting into minor but frequent scrapes. Though these would have been of little account in a rifleman, they were difficult to ignore now that R. had mounted his stripe. As a consequence he became something of a problem for me in the platoon and with my superiors, but I liked him.

When I found him on his stretcher with his head heavily bandaged, he greeted me cheerily and after we had discussed his wound and his prospects, he added with a grin, 'Anyway I shall save you some trouble for a while, sir.' Years later, when I had become a candidate for the Parliamentary constituency of Spennymoor in County Durham, I was leaving our eve of the poll meeting and was surprised to notice R. among a group of onlookers. I called out to him. 'Hullo, R. I had no idea you lived in this constituency. I thought your home was many miles away.' 'It is, sir.' And then he added with some embarrassment: 'The truth is, I heard things might be a bit rough tonight and I thought I'd better come along.'

*

As I was leaving the C.C.S. an orderly came up to me and said that an officer had seen me pass his tent door and would like to have a word with me. He was very weak and in a tent for gassed cases so would I please make it short. I approached and to my surprise found that the wounded man had been our junior major in Aldershot days, when he had sprained his ankle badly. Some careless orderly had applied the wrong ointment, blistering the skin, so that he could not walk for weeks. As a result he had been unable to sail with us but had come out some time later to join another battalion of our regiment. With one leg smashed and the other wounded, and gassed as well, he had lain for hours in no-man's-land, given up for dead, when some of our riflemen had happened upon him and brought him in. Rowley Paget looked desperately ill, but he recovered after having a leg amputated and was my neighbour in Sussex in the Second World War.

During the next fortnight few drafts reached us and only one or two officers from our reserve battalion. We were therefore tragically under strength and limited in what we could do to rest and refit our weakened companies.

I had not exaggerated my ignorance of an adjutant's duties in my reply to Foljambe, but two strokes of good fortune made all the difference for me. The first was our new colonel, as Foljambe at once became. He was an intelligent and highly trained soldier himself, and it was this which soon inspired confidence in others. He told me my duties in a few terse sentences and then left me to get on with the job. His reprimands were rare but when they came were so much in the tone of 'Well, I am no doubt the bigger fool for having made you adjutant' as to sink in all the deeper.

The riflemen came to trust him absolutely. He could be sharp-tempered but they soon learnt that Foljambe knew what he was about, that he would get them through if any man could and it was this which counted.

My second undeserved bonus was our orderly-room sergeant, Arnold Rushworth. A quiet almost hesitant demeanour concealed a quick mind and a retentive memory. My inexperienced nineteen years were over-awed by the catalogue of returns I had to submit to brigade headquarters, quite apart from the daily orders I had to give or transmit to companies. Rushworth, however, was the calm and un-hesitating master of all this and other detail. Smoothly he coped with it all, usually in conditions of muddy discomfort, and often in danger, in an over-crowded dug-out in the line. Yet I never knew him protest or express concern by more than an occasional puckered frown. He was my right hand and no small part of my brain as well.

It was only on my second day as adjutant that our brigadier came to inspect a sadly depleted battalion. General Clemson was a much-respected brigade commander. We all knew or had witnessed his quiet but unmistakable courage. He had been slightly wounded while we were at Ploegsteert, Fever-sham taking over during his absence, but had hastened his return from hospital to resume command for the Somme battles.

Being left of the line we were the last battalion for inspec-tion on what must have been for Clemson a sad tour of duty. Though our battalion and the Queen's had suffered most severely when leading the attack, the two Fusilier battalions in support had endured grievous losses also. I doubt if Clemson's brigade was at half strength that morning, even allowing for a few drafts and the reserves kept out of the last battle, so that the mood was sombre, though not stiff. It never was with Clemson.

As he walked down the line the general addressed an occasional criticism or question to the colonel or to a company commander. Listening as I followed behind them, my mind kept going back to the last such parade I had seen, the battalion at full pride and strength in Françières before leaving for the Somme. Young as I was, I felt an aching sadness. Where all were friends and volunteers, the gaps hurt the more.

Soon Clemson approached C Company with its leading platoon in weakened numbers under Sergeant Sowerby's command. His brief inspection over, the general turned to Foljambe and spoke so that the riflemen could hear: 'That is the best platoon I have seen today, colonel.' 'It was Mr

Eden's, sir,' came the quiet reply. Clemson nodded and I have never known a happier moment in my life.

Clemson could not tell us much of the future, but Foljambe was convinced that we should soon be in action again. He also thought it probable that, our casualties and those of the Queen's having been so heavy on September 15th, we could reasonably expect to be in support next time and the two Fusilier battalions in the lead. He was soon to be proved right on both counts. For the next fortnight we rehearsed assiduously the duties of a support battalion, we built strong points and we conjectured where and when our division's turn would come.

Meanwhile I had to learn my duties and in the afternoons I would delve among the mysteries of march tables, war diaries and the countless returns that officialdom demanded. First in importance among these was our casualty return for September 15th, as far as I could ascertain it. This read: *Killed*

4 officers	54 other ranks
Wounded	
10 officers	256 other ranks
Missing	70 other ranks

The missing were those of whose fate in action no survivor could give any first-hand details. As the enemy had not broken through our line at any time he could not have captured any prisoners, though as our weakened battalion was compelled to give a little ground, some of our dead remained in his hands, including the colonel. It was therefore a grim presumption that almost all the missing would be dead.

Foljambe would not allow me to stay working in our orderly-room tent every afternoon, and an occasional summons to an hour or two's riding over the down and stubble behind our camp was a welcome delight. Charlie Feversham had been a keen horseman and in addition to 'Hornpipe', a liver chestnut and a grand hunter, as his official charger, he had in reserve a strong little mare which Foljambe allotted to me instead of the poor scraggy remount which had been the adjutant's lot until then. Even so, I remained faithful to Potter's powerful horse for any jumping competitions that came along during the nine months I was still to be with the battalion. All that time we never did better than be equal first and then lose on a jump off, but Potter remained tolerant of his jockey until the end.

For himself, Foljambe preferred to keep his own thorough-bred 'Lindrick', a lovely looking light chestnut which may have been a failure as a race-horse, as we were told, but could outpace us all with ease.

Charlie had owned an Irish wolf-hound called 'Con' which was very much a one-man dog and moped miserably as the days passed and his master did not appear. Partly to exercise Con, Foljambe would take him with us and occasionally give him a run after a hare. This was not really allowed, but as we never saw a living soul, French or English, on any of our rides we soon forgot that, the more so as our activities could not conceivably have done any harm at that time of the year.

Con was rarely successful but on one of the few occasions when he was, we nearly landed in trouble. That day there were three or four of us in our party and the junior among us had to carry the dead hare, an exercise his horse did not much care about. We set off back to camp at a gentle canter when round the slope of a down we rode straight into the arms of the corps commander and his staff. Civilities were exchanged while junior contrived to handle his restless charger and conceal his burden. A glance by the general at junior and another at Con who had flopped down exhausted with his tongue hanging out, but nothing was said. However, we thought it wise to ditch poor puss before we rode into camp.

On other riding afternoons we worked to a different plan. We would put up a covey of partridges, mark it carefully, and gallop after it to put it up again and again. After a while one or two of the weaker birds in the covey would begin to flag. Then one of us would close in and, circling the tired bird on horseback, would quickly slip from the saddle and hit it over the head. By this unorthodox and dubious method we would occasionally add a brace or two of partridges to our fare.

Not long after Foljambe had taken over command, we shared in a parade of at least brigade size, perhaps larger, for some visiting authority. Rifle regiments do not fix bayonets, which they call swords, on ceremonial occasions, nor for any purpose except attacking or repelling the enemy. This is presumably a relic of North American days when the emphasis was on rapid movement rather than on display. Shortly before the visiting cavalcade approached us, a senior staff officer cantered up to Foljambe and called out, 'Fix bayonets, please, Colonel Foljambe.' 'Rifle regiments do not fix bayonets, sir,' replied Foljambe. 'Do as I say, damn it,' came the sharp rejoinder. Foljambe looked over his shoulder and gave the order: 'Fix swords.' Chaos ensued. Many of the riflemen had never practised such a drill movement in their lives, others had a faint recollection of it, so that here and there a right-hand man stepped forward and went through a caricature of the correct movement, while others just jammed their bayonets on and hoped for the best. Eventually some kind of uniformity was established, but by this time the visiting general was upon us and must have seen the confusion. I have no memory of who the visiting general was, but if he were the army commander, Rawlinson, he must have been mildly amused for he began his military career as a rifleman and was wont to say to us, 'I shall always be a rifleman at heart.' No more was heard of our little incident and no reproof was ever addressed to our colonel. We thought he deserved an apology.

*

In the first days of October we got a clear indication of what was in store for us, though detailed orders with date and time were to come through later. The brigade was to attack from a position slightly to the left and a few hundred yards in advance of the extreme limit which the battalion had reached on September 15th. This time we were to be in support, as we had expected. Foljambe was, however, a dedicated believer in reconnaissance, so that despite our secondary role in the battle he told me that we would go up the line together the next day and examine the whole layout. It was as well that we did.

We rode as far as we could and leaving horses and grooms in as much security as we were able to contrive, set off across country. There was not much risk in this and, except for some counter-battery activity, there was little to worry about until we neared a shelving incline the summit of which was being heavily and continuously shelled. 'That,' said Foljambe sourly, 'is the Gird ridge and our battalion headquarters.'

We jumped down into a communication trench and worked our way forward. It was a slow business, the trench being narrow and congested with troops moving in both directions, walking wounded, stretcher parties and occasional prisoners. The weather had broken in the last day or two and mud was beginning to add to our troubles.

At length we reached the Gird ridge and a thoroughly un-healthy place it proved to be. The trench was in poor shape, battered and open; shells seemed to be bursting everywhere and no attempt had been made to bury the enemy dead. With difficulty we found a comparatively secure bay, crouched up against the back parapet which faced the enemy and began to take a look at the country beyond, where our battalion was to deploy and support the attack. We had scarcely begun when, *thump*, and a terrific impact struck our protective parapet. It did not take us long to find out what had happened; a 5·9 shell had embedded itself in the sand-bagged wall against which we had propped ourselves, had bulged it ominously between us, but had failed to explode.

After the first moment of stunned surprise, my reaction was one of hopelessness. If this was happening to us in our first five minutes in the line, before our battle had even begun, there was no chance at all that we could win through. Perhaps sensing this, Foljambe's reaction was somewhat different. 'As we have survived that one,' he commented, 'we are evidently not going to be killed in this battle;' and he added, 'Come on, we're getting out of this.' Whereupon I scrambled after him away from our dud shell, down the forward slope of the Gird ridge and towards the front line.

Here was comparative calm. The incline was a gentle one into a valley of dead ground which extended for a good hun-dred yards, ending against a bank topped with some scruffy and shell-torn bushes. Beyond this bank lay, we knew, the opposing forward lines.

We came to a stop at the foot of the bank and looked back at the scene we had left, with the Gird ridge still enduring its remorseless bombardment. It looked very much as if the Germans expected another thrust in this sector soon.

Foljambe decided that the foot of the bank should be our headquarters from before zero hour. To my comment that we should then be in advance of our own battalion and that our companies would be attacking over us, he said that didn't matter. We would have much better contact with the battle from our bank than from the Gird ridge and we should save the lives of our runners. He added that we must do all we could to get our companies across the Gird ridge as rapidly as possible. He would speak to brigade about that. The Germans had got the range of that ridge to a 't' and it was a death-trap. We began the journey back to our camp in steadily falling rain.

During the next two days the weather grew rapidly worse. The rain never seemed to let up, so that our attack, originally fixed for October 5th, had to be postponed until the seventh, but as the weather did not improve at all, this only made matters worse. The rain had added the final touch of sordid misery to the Somme battlefield. The stench, the mud, the corpses, the destruction everywhere, the torn and twisted guns and limbers, the shattered wagons, the mutilated horses and mules created a scene of desolation beyond description. I remember one afternoon searching out our new head-quarters when suddenly I saw two of our runners, Sunderland and Iley, standing quietly under their dripping capes at the entrance to a slit trench; they looked so young and pink and white against this squalid background that for the moment I was quite startled. They seemed in such innocent contrast to their setting.

*

At about this time a circular order arrived from higher authority, it could have been corps or even army, on the subject of shell-shock. It warned against the increasing spread of this symptom and indicated that it could not be accepted for treatment as were wounds suffered in action. We knew little about this state of affairs and I could not recall a shell-shock case. Foljambe discussed the problem with our doctor who thought that from the point of view of the order we must show no sympathy, for it would no doubt be easy for the tendency to spread. I was told to instruct company commanders accordingly.

Word came that the attack was to be launched at 2 p.m. October 7th. The last stage of our approach march was a cumbersome business, Foljambe going ahead with his runner and I following with the M.O. and the main body of our headquarters for the first half of the morning under intermittent enemy shelling, which took its steady toll.

One of these random shells fell a little ahead of me and to my right where what had formerly been my company was temporarily halted. I heard a cry for stretcher-bearers and turned to find two riflemen digging out a third who had just been buried by the burst of a shell on the parapet in front of him. He proved to be Lance-Corporal S., one of our best youngsters. He had had a narrow escape and was badly concussed. He seemed dazed and to know neither where he was, nor what he should be doing. By this time the M.O., Hart, had come up and spoke to S. He told him that one of his orderlies was going down to the first-aid post and would take S. with him. The orderly would return with some supplies the doctor needed in the morning and S. was to come back with him and report to his platoon sergeant. S. seemed to have little idea what was being said to him and as I knew him as one of our keenest young N.C.O.s I began to expostulate. Hart interrupted with a warning look, saying 'Remember what the colonel told us.' I could only turn away, profoundly unhappy.

When we were out of earshot Hart added, 'I have no doubt there is nothing sham about S.'s condition, but if we had treated him as a seriously wounded case we should have done exactly what that order told us not to do. If he is better in the morning, he will want to be back on the job; if he is not, I will tell my corporal to keep him there for another twenty-four hours.'

Meanwhile Iley had been back to our transport lines to meet a small draft and his report brought me no comfort. The journey back was nearly five miles, two of these down the one and only communication trench, Turk Lane, water-logged in several places. When he reached the lines, Iley found that the new draft, about thirty all told, had just arrived. From their own account they had had no rest since leaving England about two days before and were worn out, as well as totally inexperienced in any form of war. The men were not even from our own reserve battalion. They were given some food and a short rest, and were then loaded up with the battalion's rations and started on the weary trek up the line.

Transport conditions on the Somme were appalling and the men had to travel in single file along the road. Once in Turk Lane the going was even worse, for troops and casualties were coming down all the time. It was the repeated halts because trenches were jammed, and the effort to start again for heavily burdened men, which made the use of communication trenches so mercilessly exhausting. As a result, the men straggled and Iley had to halt his party over and over again before they reached the battalion early in the morning, only to go into action that afternoon. We had allotted them to the two support companies, but even so, I heard later that only five of this new draft came through un-scathed.

Our battalion was much under strength and as the approach march dragged on through the wet and the mud, I was troubled by the casualties we were suffering. We had already lost one officer and three men killed and eight or nine wounded to my certain knowledge and there were probably more, yet we were still far from our scheduled position. I was therefore relieved when I caught up with Foljambe at our agreed rendezvous, though I found him as much concerned by the slow progress of the brigade as a whole as by our casualties. He decided that we must get ahead ourselves, and we repeated the tactics of our earlier reconnaissance, cutting across heavy and now muddied country for a spell. It was indeed Foljambe's practice never to use a trench anywhere if it were possible to move along the top. Always eager to travel quickly, he would rather chance shell-fire and bullets than be delayed.

As we trudged on Foljambe glanced at my equipment and remarked, 'Why do you wear your revolver on the wrong side?' I replied, 'I have always worn it on the left, sir, it seems easier to draw it that way.' 'Well, it's wrong,' retorted Foljambe. 'You had better change it.' I promised to do so in the future, but pleaded to be allowed to keep it as it was for the present as it would be such a business to rearrange the Christmas tree of binoculars, map-case, water-bottle, haver-sack, etc., which I was carrying. Foljambe nodded agreement, and we pressed on.

A while later I was surprised to see a subaltern from one of the battalions holding the line in advance of us walking briskly back from the front only a few yards away on our left. Signing to me to stay where I was with our runners and small headquarters staff, Foljambe walked across, stopped the young officer and was soon talking quietly but insistently to him. The boy who looked rather dazed but otherwise well enough, listened and replied and then after a pause looked again at Foljambe, turned and walked back the way he had come.

Foljambe later told me what had happened. He had asked the boy what he was doing; the reply came that he was suffer-ing from shell-shock and was on his way down the line. Foljambe asked him if he had his company commander's sanction. The subaltern replied that he had not, that he had been knocked over by a shell blast and badly shaken. His company commander had not been within reach, so that he had handed over to the nearest N.C.O. Foljambe had told him that he should not have done that and persuaded the boy to rejoin his company and try to carry on.

We reached our previously chosen headquarters under the bank without further incidents and dug for ourselves what security we could against shell-fire. At 2 p.m. our barrage came down. The German reply was immediate, on the Gird ridge and elsewhere. More serious, we could hear the crackle of machine-gun fire as the Fusilier battalions began the advance for which we were to provide close support. Our preliminary bombardment had not silenced this most deadly enemy. In a few minutes our battalion came over the ridge and down the slope towards us. It was an extraordinary sensation to watch them approach us in this way. We saw men fall, but at this stage, and in the dead ground, the casualties seemed comparatively light. B Company headquarters with two platoons on the right and D Company headquarters with two platoons on the left, were in the lead; each was to build a strong point in support of the advancing Fusiliers.

Unhappily nothing went according to plan. The afternoon attack was probably a mistake anyway. There was no element of surprise and the enemy machine-guns took deadly toll of the Fusiliers and of our riflemen also as they attempted to gain ground. It soon began to look as though our support line would become the front line, so little and irregular was our progress.

To make matters worse, shells from our own heavy artillery began to fall among us. It is easy to mistake the direction of artillery fire, but this time neither we nor the battalion headquarters on our right had any doubt about it. We each sent messages back at our speediest, but at best it must be an hour or two before the guns could be identified and given corrected orders.

Meanwhile Foljambe set off himself to make contact with D's half-company and see how it was faring. We had expected the more stubborn resistance in that sector and I was sent to make like contact with B's half-company.

Our estimate proved mistaken. D Company had suffered heavy casualties, but it had reached its objective and was building its strong-point under its company commander's energetic guidance. This was Geoffrey Sheardown, a very tough and experienced officer.

B Company was in much worse plight. Enemy machine-guns were constantly active, and it was not easy to form a true picture of what was happening. At the outset I walked into a stretcher party bearing one of the most intelligent of our young officers. He had only joined us a short while before.

I asked him where he had been hit and he looked up at me, smiled and said a little ruefully, 'In the stomach.' We both remembered how a few nights before some of us had been discussing, as was common enough in a Somme interlude, where we would prefer to be hit. Each had his preference, an arm, a shoulder, a leg; we had all agreed that the stomach was the one to be feared. Next day I learnt that Anderson had died before reaching the casualty clearing station.

Anderson was typical of the best of our volunteers. He was short-sighted and no doctor would have passed him under any serious test. No doubt he had ducked that somehow. He was an intellectual and an excellent company officer. By a chance which I would never have dreamt possible in 1916, I became many years later the friend and colleague of his uncle, Walter Runciman.

It is remarkable how many of those who would certainly not have been dubbed by their schoolmaster athletic or of strong physical constitution volunteered and then showed exceptional courage. I remember a boy at my private school who was about half-way in age between my brother Timothy and myself. My mother and his mother were friends, so that we exchanged an occasional sentence in that rather em-barrassed fashion which boys use when told by parents to be kind to each other. He was tall for his age and clever, but also physically weak and ungainly. His limbs seemed hard to control so that he ran clumsily and was no good at games in a school where their importance was overrated. He can hardly have been happy there. When the war came he joined a Welsh line regiment and won a posthumous V.C. for a deed of cool and outstanding bravery.

*

As I continued to explore with Iley the ground where B Company should have advanced in support of the Fusiliers, I began to understand the tragic plight of both units. Their losses from machine-gun fire had been cruel, there were dead and wounded fusiliers and riflemen everywhere. Just as I was wondering where I could find a surviving officer, a very young lance-corporal emerged from nowhere, stood sharply to attention and reported, 'Lance-Corporal X in charge of

B Company, sir.' Nearby, he explained, were six riflemen, the only survivors of B Company he had been able to collect, apart from a few who were helping the stretcher-bearers get some of the badly wounded back to the first-aid post. As they could not build the strong-point where they had been ordered, he had put his surviving riflemen to dig a support trench from which they could command some field of fire and was about to make a wider sweep of ground to see if he could find any others. He believed that the half-company's officers and senior N.C.O.s had all been killed or wounded.

I was impressed and moved by this boy's report and told him how well he had done. We then moved off together, said a word of encouragement to his riflemen and began our wider sweep. It was soon all too evident how bad the situation was. There were only a few survivors and these were in scattered handfuls, far apart and scarcely able to move under the intense machine-gun fire. Most of the casualties appeared to have taken place either during the short advance or during gallant but vain attempts to take on the securely entrenched German machine-gunners. For whatever reason, the barrage had not knocked them out.

We had nearly finished our task and the autumn day was beginning to fade when we found yet another batch of wounded, including B Company commander, Claud Burton. He spoke cheerfully enough but his voice was feeble and he looked pale and weak. He had been wounded early in the attack and could add nothing to what we knew, but he had refused to be carried down sooner, declaring that the more seriously wounded must go first, which was typical of this modest and gentle man. Now his turn had come, but the wait had chilled him to the bone, so that I laid my British-warm on him with instructions to the stretcher-bearers to return it later.

I decided that I must get back to Foljambe at once. The situation was stark enough in its grim reality for there to be little doubt what we had to do. We must bring up at least the other half of B Company and perhaps one of our reserve companies to reinforce the weakened right against a possible counter-attack; we must bring some order among the scattered pockets of fusiliers and riflemen against that threat and we must organize some means of getting our many wounded away during the night. In our one narrow and crowded communication trench the stretchers had often to be raised above the top of the parapet and the zigzag journey back to the nearest point an ambulance could reach might take four men eight hours for one casualty, sometimes with fatal results.

It must have been about this time that I looked down at my revolver holster and saw with surprise that it was badly gashed. A portion of the leather had been torn through, evidently by a piece of the shrapnel which the Germans had been bursting over us with uncomfortable regularity all the afternoon. Next to the machine-gun it was our most deadly enemy in this battle. When, later on, I showed my testimony to Foljambe, he agreed that I should keep my revolver on the wrong side, for the rest of the war if I wanted to.

I found Foljambe under our bank when I got back. He gave me orders to report at once to brigade headquarters about the serious condition of the wounded of whom we could not hope to move more than a fraction by our stretcher-bearers. Orders were sent to reinforce our right with the remnants of B and some of A Company, while Foljambe went himself to straighten out intermingled riflemen and fusiliers there and build a defensible position. I was instructed to tell the battalion we were supporting and brigade headquarters what Foljambe was doing.

It was not until afterwards that I learnt, not from Foljambe, how exacting his task had been. With darkness falling and after a hard day's fighting with heavy losses, Foljambe had to impose his will on a force of mixed units where surviving officers and N.C.O.s sometimes did not know him, order them to take up new positions and dig themselves in against the counter-attack which could be expected at dawn. In this he had little help and richly earned the D.S.O. which was later awarded to him. During the night we also dug a communication trench on our left forward to Sheardown's strong-point which was by now the most advanced portion of the line.

We manned our bank at stand-to for the expected counter-attack. Sure enough, as dawn was breaking a number of men loomed up almost straight ahead, moving steadily towards us. From the noise they made we judged them to be about company strength. They would overwhelm us with ease, I reflected, as I waited for Foljambe's order to fire. I thought that he had delayed too long when out of the mist called an unmistakably English voice. Foljambe replied and the interlopers were soon identified as a working party under a junior brigade staff officer who had lost their way in the mist and darkness. They had done no good but had fortunately suffered little loss. We briefed them as to the position on our front and sent them on their way, emphasizing again that we must have help with the wounded that day or most of them would be dead of exposure by nightfall.

Probably they gave their message effectively. In any event in the afternoon a party of Durham Light Infantry under an R.A.M.C. officer arrived with stretchers to help us get our wounded away. I can still remember my intense delight when I realized what these military Samaritans had come to do. During the night we had concentrated on getting most of the wounded back into the dead ground so the work went ahead without respite.

That evening, October 8th, some changes were made in the dispositions of the brigade with the result that our battalion, now very weak in numbers and especially in officers and senior N.C.O.s, was drawn back into the Gird trench and Gird support. Our battalion headquarters moved to Factory Corner. Under this battered building, of which nothing but rubble remained, were some quite strong cellars, which could at a pinch accommodate two battalion headquarters with their staff and signallers. But this was no unmixed blessing. The site was well known to the Germans who had used the factory cellars themselves and as a result they kept up an almost continuous bombardment of the approaches. Getting in and out was no picnic for us or our runners, and still less for the signallers whose dangerous job it was to mend the wires which were broken again and again. I had much preferred our bank.

We remained in these positions through October 9th, but were greatly astonished when orders arrived that we were to send back guides to meet drafts for our battalion. They were to be expected that afternoon and were to be allotted to platoons and companies. This was the first we had heard of drafts for us being even at the base. We had hoped for news of some from our reserve battalion between the two Somme battles when they would have been invaluable, but could learn nothing.

Now it would be impossible to make any intelligent attempt to integrate these drafts into what was left of the battalion when we were in the line and under constant shell-fire. The drafts themselves would not be given half a chance. Added to all this the method of handling the business made us feel that we might next be called upon to make another attack based on the argument that the battalion had now been strengthened. With large numbers, perhaps a majority of recruits who, however brave, had never had any battle experience, we could obviously do no such thing.

I sent Iley back with the guides, for I knew that with his bump of locality and cool courage he could get these drafts through to us if any man could. Late that night Iley reported to me and it was a woeful tale he had to tell. The men were not from our reserve battalion or indeed from our regiment at all. They had enlisted as volunteers in an Eastern counties regiment and were naturally astonished to find themselves amongst us.

Worse than that, as Iley reported, they were excusably bewildered and alarmed at being led up to and through some of the heaviest artillery fire the war had seen so far. Laden with our rations, which they had been ordered to bring up with them, some of them showed a strong and natural preference to rest a while at the bottom of a communications trench, using the ration bags as head cover.

For Iley and his fellow guides this was all a new and harrowing experience, as it was for the unfortunate drafts themselves. We did what we could to divide them up intelligently, but in those conditions it had to be a crash job.

It was, I think, the next day that Foljambe was summoned

to brigade headquarters, apparently for a conference of battalion commanders. Probably it was then, or maybe by an earlier message, that Foljambe expressed himself vigorously about the possibility of mounting a further attack, at least so far as our battalion was concerned. He made it firmly clear that the troops he commanded, with the new drafts arrived only a few hours before, were in no condition to take part in another offensive at that time. Whether such a project was ever contemplated by higher authority we never knew, but there were strong rumours of it, and that Foljambe's blunt negative had put an end to it. Instead, we received orders that we should be relieved the next night by the Seventeenth Manchester Regiment and the Second Battalion, the Royal Scots, which was in itself a confusing business for one battalion lamentably under strength.

As we were preparing to leave, without regret, our head-quarters at Factory Corner, the commanding officer of the Fusilier battalion with whom we had been sharing the space spoke to Foljambe of the exemplary conduct of one of his subalterns, how he had rallied his men in conditions of the utmost danger, adding that this subaltern was due to report at battalion headquarters at any time now and that he would like Foljambe to meet him.

A few moments later there was a clatter on the cellar steps and there emerged from the semi-darkness the young officer of Foljambe's encounter a few mornings before. Foljambe congratulated him warmly and the subaltern and I exchanged cheerful grins. Had I been a little older I might have reflected on the many facets of courage. Foljambe was genuinely delighted.

Earlier that afternoon a gunner officer called in at Factory Corner. Having identified our unit he gave us unexpected tidings. On his way back from a forward observation post he had come upon the body of a dead officer which closer inspection showed to be that of a lieutenant-colonel in a rifle regiment, who he thought had been killed about a month before. He showed us on his map where he judged that the body lay.

Foljambe thanked the officer and assured him that a party

would be detailed to bury Lord Feversham that night. He then told me that he must stay with the battalion during the relief operation and that I should take charge of a small search and burial party and set out just as dawn was breaking. We were pretty confident from the map reference and the lie of the land that we could not be spotted by the enemy; but if we were, and the enemy started shelling us heavily, I was to give up. We must not run foolhardy risks of incurring more casualties.

I selected Sergeant Jim Dale, our pioneer sergeant, who had been brought up on the Feversham estate and who was devoted to Charlie, Bob Iley and two other riflemen. Dale contrived during the night to make a small wooden cross from material he had got hold of, I don't know where, and had carved Charlie's name on it.

We set out at our appointed hour and soon found what I judged to be our map reference, but despite a detailed search of the ground we failed to find the body. It was now getting light and some desultory dawn shelling began to fall rather too close. I therefore decided that we should make one more sweep, this time a little wider than the previous ones and, if we failed, we would have to give up.

At first this fared no better, but just as I was deciding that I must accept failure, one of our party, I think it was Sergeant Dale, who was furthest forward, called out that he had found the colonel. Then I understood that Charlie had led his men even further towards the enemy lines on that September 15th than we had thought possible. His body lay on the forward slope of a lip in the ground where he had fallen, as his and Oakley's weakened battalions advanced upon that 'next objective', still virtually intact. Sadly we set about our task. I read a few lines from the burial service, which someone had lent to me at headquarters, Dale set up the wooden cross, we gave our commanding officer a last salute and turned away, leaving him to Picardy and the shells.

X

The Spirit of Man

The next few days were miserable. We moved from one camp site to another, wet and disheartened at the failure of our battle and the loss of so many friends; for that is what the Yeoman Rifles of all ranks were, just friends, and it was now borne in upon us that the Yeoman Rifles as such had ceased to exist. Two Somme battles had seen to that. On October 2nd we went into the line twelve officers and 350 other ranks. We came out on the night of October 8th six officers and 170 other ranks. The losses were more severe than these figures show, because our strength when we were relieved included the survivors among the drafts which had reached us during these days and nights.

An additional complication in the October fighting was the delay in communication with brigade headquarters which, as Foljambe commented, was too far behind the line. Wires having been repeatedly cut by shell-fire, despite all that our signallers could do, the only sure means of contact was by runner, but our strength in runners was limited and reduced by casualties. Yet it was imperative to keep in touch also with companies and neighbouring battalions. One can only suppose that this distant stationing of headquarters was due to an error of judgment compounded by the worsening weather, which further stretched the journey for our runners. In any event, during the ten days of our approach march and the battle, I never saw an officer from brigade headquarters except the junior who had strayed into our lines.

Nor did we see anyone from divisional headquarters, which was less surprising. This did not go unnoticed by the riflemen. Some weeks later two of them were on local leave walking across a square in a town behind the Ypres Salient, when the divisional commander and his staff rode glittering by. The general stopped to speak to our men and asked them which battalion of the regiment they were serving with. When they told him he added, 'Good, and were you with me on the Somme?' to which one of them replied, 'We did not see you there, sir.' A good rifleman's story maybe, but it expressed the inner thoughts of many.

At this distance of time it is not easy to estimate why the heavy casualties, mud and failure did not have a more enduring effect on men's spirits. The answer that all were volunteers is not enough and a combination of other factors must be added, including the evidence we saw of enemy losses, captured prisoners and the unshakeable conviction of final victory. Political figures were not discussed and certainly not liked. Lloyd George was the most generally accepted and those campaigning against conscription the most condemned.

Fricourt was the first staging post on the way back from the line, nothing but ruins and a notice board. We had been there before, after our battalion's first battle on the Somme, and the riflemen had no love for it. Conditions were so bad that the last men back from the battle had to doss down in pairs by spreading out one groundsheet and lying on it, then pulling up the second man's sheet to cover the two of them. All this in unceasing pouring rain. Early on the morning of October 11th I reported to the colonel that we had found Charlie's body and buried it.

Later that morning we began four days of shunting about in cattle trucks and marching, Fricourt, Bécordelle, Buire. Here we had hoped for a breathing spell to re-form our battalion, but we were only given forty-eight hours. On one of the days Foljambe held a battalion parade. He spoke to us briefly and simply, as he knew so well how to do, and welcomed the large new draft which had arrived in the line after the battle. Wisely he attempted no drill, for the newcomers could know nothing of our practices and these would have to be taught by stages. This is how Bob Iley saw it:

We moved back to Allery, tidied up, checked on casualties and began to receive reinforcements. Our drafts were composed principally of Londoners and it was wonderful how they were absorbed. At first they were strange to us in every way. We had different expressions. Our Durham lads asked, what do they call you, they said, what's your name. They used the word Bastard almost as a sign of affection. To us it was the most insulting word they could use. Almost all our N.C.O.s were new to their ranks but they all had the same background. Our standards remained and it was wonderful living and working with these Londoners and seeing them adopt our ways and become part of us.

The official war diary which I was keeping as adjutant at the time briefly records the shunting movements which followed:

AIRAINES 16/10/16. Battalion proceeded by train from Edge Hill siding to Airaines.

17/10/16. Battalion detrained at Airaines and marched to billets at Allery.

ALLERY 18/10/16. The battalion remained in billets at Allery and the day was spent in reorganizing companies and specialists.

19/10/16. Battalion marched to Longpres-les-Corps-Saints station and entrained at 3.51 a.m. (20/10/16).

METEREN 20/10/16. The battalion detrained at Caestre and marched to billets in farm near Meteren.

VICTORIA CAMP 21/10/16. The battalion marched from Meteren to Victoria Camp M.3.C.S.S.

These restless and uncomfortable movements led us to a final destination: the sector of the line we were to occupy that winter of 1916–17. This lay on the southern flank of the Ypres Salient, opposite the Bois Carré, with, not so far to its north, St Eloi, the scene of much bitter fighting in the first and second battles of Ypres. The name was also familiar to me because a young Auckland cousin, Bill Eden, much praised in my Eton days, had been killed there with my regiment.

We soon settled down to the inevitable routine of our new sector, having relieved the Australians. Loose was the word that seemed to fit these troops. Physically strong but loosely built in contrast with our stockier types, looser in the outer shows of discipline yet with an instinct for battle, brilliantly led by the ablest soldier of the war, General Monash, it is no surprise that the enemy had rather be anywhere else in the world than facing the Anzacs.

Six days in the line, followed by six in support in Ridge Wood, six more back in the line and then the same period at 'rest' in a camp at La Clytte, became our established pattern.

For the first few weeks our enemies were mud and rats and then for the rest of the winter icy cold and rats, for this proved to be one of the harshest winters in Flanders' history. The issue of mittens for the hands and whale oil for the feet gave little comfort. For our toll of casualties, the cold was both good and bad. The sodden condition of our line and the German command of the higher ground in the Ypres area, which enabled them to drain their trenches into ours, made it impossible to dig to any depth. Our defences, therefore, were all built-up parapets with a propensity for slithering into the mud. The frost sealed all this. On the other hand the impact of the enemy shells could be deadened in the mud, while fragments from a burst on frozen ground would travel far and dangerously. Either way, life for the companies in the line was very hard that winter. Fuel was short and water, and so was a hot meal.

Conditions at battalion headquarters near the old Brasserie were slightly better, but not the rats. My mother had sent me out a handsome box of chocolate peppermint creams from Morrell Brothers, Cobbett and Son, the fashionable confectioner of those days. I decided to keep it for Christmas and so put the box on a rough shelf at the foot of my bunk in the dug-out with Con, the wolf-hound, sleeping on the floor beside it. In the morning every single chocolate in the box had been nibbled and we never tasted one. These rats were more like buck rabbits in size, revolting to sight and touch. Even Con had soon been sated, which perhaps explained why the chocolates went undefended. That was altogether a bad Christmas gastronomically. Our headquarters cook had contrived to make a Christmas pudding for the riflemen at headquarters and just as his task was done, down dropped a shell on the cookhouse, blowing it to pieces, though miraculously without serious casualties other than the dinner.

More enduring was a copy of Robert Bridge's *The Spirit of Man*, sent to me by my cousin Violet Dickinson who alone among my family had an unerring instinct for the present which would delight one most. Years later she was to give me a pair of elegant eighteenth-century silver-gilt taper sticks, which had once belonged to William Pitt's only love, Eleanor Eden. Meanwhile, the Bridges anthology, which naturally contained much that was a revelation to a nineteen-year-old boy, made a perfect retreat for the sensibilities. Battered now, it has a place still in my library.

Less successful was another venture, prompted not by politics but by literature. I ordered a Russian grammar from home. For some reason nearly all the translations of Russian writers in those days, at least in the Windlestone library, were into French. The single exception was Constance Garnett's brilliant translations of Turgenev. In my last visits to Windlestone and encouraged by my father, I had broken into the Russian novelists who soon proved a joyous revelation to me. It was then that I made up my mind to read them in their own language. Even an adjutant could find time heavy on his hands in winter in Flanders. My plan was to snatch at least an hour's study every day and in addition to learn by heart some grammar exercise every morning while shaving. I persevered for many weeks but had then to accept disappointment at my slow rate of progress. Even so, I did not lose interest and when in post-war Oxford languages were being considered for a degree, the Slav group was high in favour and only second to the Persian and Arabic of my final choice.

*

For the adjutant, perhaps the most exacting task that winter was the nightly visit of inspection to companies in the line. On the whole I preferred the moonlit nights despite the need for more care against snipers. The use of a torch was forbidden, and it was my duty to dowse verbally any torches I saw, though on a dark night it could be a question of flashing a light or breaking one's neck.

Life in close support in Ridge Wood was relatively easier, despite the penetrating cold against which there was little protection. We lived for the most part in trenches and dug-outs with the occasional heavily sandbagged hut, but wood was so scarce that the only effective method of heating was by means of the famous Bairnsfather brazier. This had its limitations even when we had the charcoal, the fumes soon becoming poisonous in the cramped quarters of a dug-out. Even so, when the sector was quiet Ridge Wood was tolerable, only marred by the endless working parties up the line with their dreary duties. We would protest to brigade about these, usually without success.

Murrumbidgee camp at La Clytte, to which we were withdrawn one week in four, was an unfriendly place, deep in mud and with a scarcity of duckboards, so that we all had to plunge from hut to hut, cold and windswept when the frosts came. Despite the discomfort the camp was rarely shelled and we were in reserve and could relax to some extent. It is true that we were under orders to reinforce the front line if required, but this contingency seemed remote and I can only recall one summons in the six months we occupied the sector. That came, of course, at an ill-chosen moment. The officers were being entertained in the sergeants' mess, which was apt to be quite an evening; while the runners had seized the occasion to strip and bathe with the help of a few buckets of water. Our communications system was not therefore at its strongest. However, the runners maintained that, within a minute, they were on their way to companies and trans-port. Certain it is that the battalion was soon marshalled and on the move over the inevitable Flanders *pavé*, even if here and there equipment was in disarray and its wearer con-fused. Fortunately we had not progressed very far when word came that the Fusiliers had repulsed their attackers and we could return to our camp.

For a very young and inexperienced adjutant the brigade headquarters, and especially the brigade major, with whom he has to deal perhaps several times a day, is one of the pivots of his existence. I was therefore doubly fortunate in our newly-appointed brigade major. A sapper named Leng, he was cool, quick and professionally efficient. Looking back on those days, I think he must also have been exceptionally patient for I soon felt that he was a friend to whom I could turn in any emergency. There were plenty of these in the coming months and I had scores of occasions to be grateful to him.

Our move into the Ypres area also had some consequences for us in the higher command. Though we changed our corps sectors from time to time, for these were generally geographical, we were for most of the next eight months in Tenth Corps, commanded by General Morland, himself an officer in the Sixtieth whom we respected and liked. He was a human as well as a very competent commander who would not, however, smile upon eccentricities in battalions of his own regiment, as we were soon to learn. One or two of our officers thought it might be original to complement our black buttons with the wearing of a black tie; perhaps they even thought that the corps commander as a rifleman might tolerate this sartorial novelty. They were soon undeceived by a tart order forbidding the practice and adding that the corps commander did not permit fancy dress in his corps.

Even more important than the corps was the Army Command, though for some months we were not to know why. We were now back in the Second Army under General Plumer, the man who knew the Ypres Salient best. At a superficial glance Plumer with his eye-glass, medium height, somewhat portly figure and runaway chin, might not be impressive; but watch his methods for a while or hear him speak and you would soon know that here was the skilled and painstaking commander who was master of every detail of his job. A man to be trusted.

After the victory at Messines in the summer of 1917 it was said that Plumer was asked to what he attributed his success. He replied quietly, 'Perhaps because I am an infantryman, and this is an infantryman's war.'

Plumer knew our battalion and its history well: we had been under his command at Plugstreet Wood and Feversham had been a close friend from the days not so long ago when the general had commanded Northern Command at home.

On arrival in January for one of our early spells at La Clytte, we received a message that the army commander would pay us an informal visit the next day. This was to be treated as a normal rest day with no special parades. The general, we were told, would inspect the camp, which proved to be a characteristically thorough Plumer exercise. He had brought with him his senior 'Q' staff officer and Royal Engineer. We were first questioned as to the arrangements we had made for the stationing and care of the men's weapons and equipment in their huts, their food, their baths, their clean clothing; then the inspection began of every hut and every building in the camp. Plumer found much of which he did not approve and clear, firm orders were given to his staff on the action to be taken to mend matters. Nor did I escape entirely. Looking into one hut, Plumer commented, 'I thought you said rifles were to be slung, in this hut they are piled. How do you explain that, Mr Eden?' Mr Eden could not and was told to ensure that the orderly officer had the necessary instructions immediately.

For the riflemen, especially for the few survivors of the battalion he had known, Plumer had kindly words. He would ask them about present conditions or sometimes recall the small north country towns or villages which were their homes, while the later recruits watched and marvelled at this general who seemed so much at ease and interested in them and their cookhouses. The next day things began to happen, with a luxurious clatter of duckboards in the lead.

Thereafter we entered those long periods of cold monotony laced with funk which was trench warfare in winter.

*

There was so much waiting in the trenches. Waiting through the hour before dawn for stand-down, waiting for the battalion which was to relieve us, waiting for rations and for letters, waiting for leave, or the blighty wound, or. . .

Almost any variation was welcome, provided it stirred no significant retaliation. There was one such which impressed us for its international courtesy. Our battalion front was covered by our own divisional artillery, and by a Belgian battery of sixty pounders. The officers of this unit were always considerate enough to send a message a few moments before they opened fire, followed by another when their shelling was over. This gave us just enough time to warn our companies before the inevitable retaliation followed, thereby probably saving us several casualties during the winter. Not surprisingly our relations with our considerate defenders continued to be friendly.

One of the depressants of that winter of 1916–17 was our failure to get reinforcements from our reserve battalion, and my own to persuade the base to send us young subalterns whom I knew and who had expressed a wish to join us. Each of them had been commissioned into the regiment. One had Yorkshire parents who had written to us and seemed particularly suitable; but no, he was drafted to another battalion and was killed a few weeks after arrival. Two others, both contemporaries whom I made a special effort to get, one in my O.T.C. training squad at Eton and the other a Winchester scholar, also failed to reach us and were killed within a few months. I never pretended even to myself that they would necessarily have lived longer with us; but when you are very young and in an adventure that may mean death at any hour, it is good to see again a face you know. I could not forget nor easily forgive my failures.

Equally unhappy was the experience of House, our butler at Windlestone, who had joined the ranks of our reserve battalion. After the battle of the Somme, when, reduced to a handful of survivors, we were clamouring for reinforcements from that specially enlisted volunteer reserve, he was drafted to a regiment of which he knew nothing, and which knew nothing of him. In this he shared the fate of the overwhelming majority of all ranks from our reserve battalion who were scattered among a variety of units where the drill and traditions they had learnt were only an embarrassment to them. Although the men were all volunteers, this was an almost constant experience of ours, and no doubt of others, in the First World War, causing much unnecessary unhappiness. Men prefer to fight, and fight better, in the company they have chosen.

Soon after the New Year, periods of leave for home began

to come round and I determined to divide mine between London and Windlestone. This gave me the chance to see something of my sister Marjorie which I longed to do. Her husband, Guy, had been wounded in the thigh and hand while commanding a Canadian brigade during the Somme battles. The hand wound in particular was still being treated during my leave. We saw friends and plays and gossiped and I called on Charlie's mother, Lady Helmsley, whom I had known all my short life; she was the sister of our neighbour, Lady Londonderry. Foljambe had warned me to be careful in what I said, because Lady Helmsley was much upset by the circumstances of Charlie's death and by what she had learned from some of the wounded. There was nothing to be gained by creating more unhappiness. I cannot now recall the details of the interview, but probably it was in the main about the finding of Charlie's body and its burial.

Altogether, I did not feel entirely at home in war-time London. Everybody was extremely kind to me personally and asked the expected questions about one's experiences. Perhaps it was a mingled sense of bustle and a certain glittering unreality that bewildered me, so that I was not sorry to take the train for the North. Here I found a Windlestone transformed into a V.A.D. hospital, but it seemed a cheerful place and I enjoyed every minute of my stay. I found one or two of our riflemen among the wounded, including Dent who had been in my own No. 9 Platoon and, as old soldiers at the age of nineteen, we had much to tell each other.

My brother Jack's horses were still in the stables, including a favourite of mine, 'Carpenter', so that I could ride as often as I wished. Our local fox-hounds still met from time to time, but the only day I could reach them was nearly a disaster. It was foggy and probably the hounds should have been taken home, but our secretary, partly I think out of kindness to me, for he knew it was my only chance of a day's hunting, decided to draw a covert in our best 'Friday' country. The field was not more than half a dozen at most. We soon found and managed with difficulty to keep up with hounds which were travelling at a good pace in the fog and it was only at a check that we suddenly realized we had no more than half-a-dozen couple of hounds with us. There had been a second fox and it was some time later that we found the huntsman with the rest of the pack. As the railway main line ran not too far away, we had some anxious moments before the pack was reunited, for there were prize-winning hounds among them and they were the special care and interest of our master who was not out that day.

Despite these contrasts and my joy at being home again, when I stood at the ha-ha and looked across to the elm tree my father had painted so often, and beyond to the rolling countryside, I wondered if ever again I could see them free from the memory of those other, shell-torn trees, twisted wire and heaped and silent bodies.

*

I never became used to the departure of leave trains. It was not just fear and dislike of a return to war, though these were strong; it was, I suppose, the pent-up emotion, all the harder to endure because it was pent-up, of those who bravely came to say good-bye. There was only Marjorie left of our family to see me off and she understood that I would rather be alone, but these poignant farewells did teach me one lesson which in my selfishness I had overlooked. Whatever we youngsters may have felt about returning to battle, we had no claim to sympathy compared with the married officer. For him and his wife it really did hurt, with an added haunting fear if they had young children and the soldier, sailor or airman were the breadwinner. Theirs was the true courage.

Time brings its changes, even in the trenches, and in January we had suffered an unexpected blow, from promotion, not war. Foljambe had been ordered back to England to instruct at a school for commanding officers. He was an admirable choice for the job and he had certainly earned a break, but the battalion and particularly its adjutant were desolate. Foljambe was an excellent trainer of men. As second-in-command and our senior regular soldier, he had been chiefly responsible for the battalion's earlier instruction and, since the devastating Somme casualties, it had been his practised hand which had patiently and thoroughly reshaped us into an effective fighting unit once again. I could not imagine how we could keep the momentum going without him. We just did not know enough. For myself I was miserable at parting with the man I so much admired and who had taught me all I knew. Foljambe's cool, firm efficiency, his intelligent dedication to the job in hand and his refusal to be put off by pretexts, however plausible, set me standards at an impressionable age, so that at least I knew what I ought to have done even when I failed.

The principal gain to balance against Foljambe's departure was the beginning of a trickle, from December onwards, of our returning wounded. These were a splendid reinforcement, each one of them, we felt, being worth two of the ordinary recruit. There would have been more, but a proportion accepted commissions in other units; altogether nearly two hundred were given to N.C.O.s and riflemen in our battalion in its less than three years of life.

For myself the highlight was the reappearance of Eddie Worsley who had been wounded leading A Company in our first Somme battle. Eddie was exactly the man we needed. With a caustic tongue and occasional biting wit, he never let anything perturb him. If there was ever a comic side to any military order or activity he could be trusted to find it and chuckle over it when we were alone. Add to this a simple, direct courage and a quick mind and it did not take us long to learn how fortunate we should be in our new second-in-command.

As the weeks of that long winter and late spring dragged by, Worsley and our much-loved doctor Alan Hart became close friends. Despite their geographically distant backgrounds, Eton and Oxford for Eddie and excellent Canadian schooling for Doc, the two men had much in common. Both affected an outward cynicism, especially where military hocus-pocus was concerned, yet both were scrupulously conscientious down to the smallest details in their own duties, which were discharged as not worth a mention. Both were quick to detect and praise the work of others, especially their juniors. They shared a deeply sincere if lightly expressed admiration for our volunteer riflemen and loved to tell stories of their comments and adventures. Yet Worsley had already been twice wounded and Hart was to receive an over-earned Military Cross for much more than duty done, without thought of rest or risk, among the casualties of the Somme. Both men did me a power of good without my being mature enough to understand it, and we three soon established a triumvirate at headquarters which helped to make life tolerable, even at cut-throat bridge.

*

Foljambe's successor, Talbot Jarvis, came from our own brigade where he had been commanding our senior battalion, the Tenth Queen's Regiment. We had heard something of his almost legendary reputation for courage during the Somme battles. One of the tales told of him was that he was standing one day at the top of the steps at Factory Corner viewing the desolation around him, about as unhealthy a spot for contemplation as could be imagined. The inevitable shell burst and a piece of shrapnel hit him over the heart, tumbling him down the steps. For most men this would have been the end, but not for Jarvis. Helped to his feet, he felt in his left hand top tunic pocket from which, embedded in a pad of official papers which had no business to be there, he extracted from the last document which alone had not been pierced, that homing piece of shrapnel.

There was something fatherly in Jarvis's feeling towards his battalion. He cared sincerely for its well-being in every sense. He was a brewer by profession and his attitude towards us had in it something of the benevolent chairman of a prosperous company which runs a successful profit-sharing scheme. He wanted each one of us to do well and wherever possible he wanted our riflemen to be rewarded for it. For instance, he was generous about commissions. This was always a difficult question for company commanders and for the adjutant. We were pressed from time to time to name candidates for commissions. Depleted as our ranks had been by the Somme casualties, this was a vexing dilemma. We wanted to do justice to the claims, often strong ones, of our best N.C.O.s and riflemen, but the strongest candidates could least be spared.

Jarvis did not share our hesitation and ruled that there

must be no holding back. From the point of view of the army he was of course right, but from the battalion's we found it hard and only won occasional relief when, as sometimes happened, a candidate firmly refused the proffered nomination.

Every combatant soldier knows how chancy is the whole business of decorations. Feversham and Foljambe had put forward their recommendations with chequered success, as was normal. Jarvis, however, was more combative and if he did not get his way would return to the charge with vigour and argument. Some would doubt if the reward repaid the effort, but that was not how Jarvis saw it. For him, here was one more cause to champion on behalf of the men he was responsible for, like ensuring that their rations were never skimped and that they were not put upon for more than their share of working parties.

When the battalion was in action Jarvis could become something of a problem. His constant effort was to get into battle personally. He was impatient at waiting with battalion headquarters, even momentarily, to see how events developed. In the early stages of the Messines battle, for instance, the colonel had, unknown to me, ordered Iley to come with him to get some Germans out of a dug-out. The runner had at the moment no weapon in his hand except a Very pistol, presumably because as orderly at our headquarters he had just fired some signal in connection with our advance. However, he pointed this at the enemy, who were anyway much too shaken by the mine explosion to offer any resistance, the capture was concluded and the colonel delighted. Sometimes the adjutant had to discourage these enterprises, not least because a sense of direction was not our commanding officer's strong point. Eddie Worsley was a tower of strength on these occasions, but under the new rules, which rightly kept seconds-in-command out of action, he was not often around. All of which seemed to a nineteen-year-old adjutant to leave him too much responsibility, with a colonel who was lion-hearted but not adaptable and liable to be put out by the unexpected. But then the young adjutant probably took himself too seriously.

I soon grew to like Jarvis, for he understood my devotion to Foljambe, whom he had also respected. The trouble was that he just could not accept danger while I was only too conscious of it. To me each bursting shell was that much more unendurable than its predecessor. We had now been in the line on and off, with precious little off, for almost a year and so far from having become a seasoned warrior, and therefore increasingly impervious to danger, I felt exactly the opposite and hated with growing fervour the whole business of being shot at, whether by shell or machine-gun, but particularly shell. What depressed me most was that I could see no hope of improvement ahead. Our rests did not seem to make things any better except maybe for a day, but I knew that I was not alone and that in varying degrees most of us had to live with the same incubus.

Courage can take so many forms. Most men can be brave once in their lives and there are others who never seem conscious of danger. It may be tempting to account for these as lacking imagination, but it need not be true. There have been men who could discipline themselves to be insensitive to danger and who lacked neither brains nor imagination. In my experience Walter Moyne was one of these. I happened to succeed him as brigade major in the last year of the war when he took over as G.S.O.2 of our division. Inevitably our work threw us much together and we became friends. On one occasion, I would guess in the early autumn of 1918, we were walking down a road deep in discussion about some future plan Walter had brought to me, when I noticed that about 200 yards ahead the Germans were shelling heavily a cross-roads we were approaching. We continued to walk, Walter to expound and I to listen. I began to look anxiously at the shelled cross-roads, for it was a frequent practice of the Germans at this late period of the war to mine important cross-roads as they retreated and then to shell them to prevent their being repaired. Walter made no sign, but I could bear it no longer and stopped in my tracks with the comment: 'I don't know, Walter, whether you intend walking into that barrage, but I am against it.' Walter surveyed the scene, as it were for the first time. 'Oh yes,' he said, 'they do seem to be shelling quite heavily. What do you suggest?' 'I suggest,' I replied, 'that we go round and rejoin the road beyond the shelling.' Walter agreed readily enough, but I wondered to myself, what would he have done if he had been alone with his thoughts.

Of all the variants of courage there is one which in my judgment surpasses all. The bomb disposal squads, whether in London in the blitz or in Ulster more recently, are surely the bravest of men. In cold blood calmly to place your life at a desperate hazard in the hope of saving others can never be surpassed and rarely equalled by any deed of daring or even sacrifice in the heat of battle.

XI

Crater Lane

With the coming of spring in 1917, millions of young men's thoughts had to turn to battle, ours among them. We had little doubt that we should be taking part in an offensive somewhere, the question was, where and when. We knew nothing, but the daily conjecture, canvassed with mixed feelings, at least made a break in our monotony. The prevalent opinion was that we should be moved south again. Our chief reason for expecting such a decision was that the conditions for an offensive in the Ypres Salient were so bad, with the Germans able to observe every move of a battery or a platoon, that an attack in this area hardly seemed feasible.

At the end of March we came out of the line. Bob Iley describes how we were relieved:

As we left the Ridge Wood sector, I was sent to meet the commanding officer of the incoming troops. He was a charming man and asked me about the line. I told him it was nice and quiet but that we had filled one cemetery and were well on to filling another, that rations had to be carried across country as the Vierstraat Road was heavily shelled etc. Captain Eden gave me a smart telling off for trying to put the wind up a D.S.O. with a record of hard fighting in France and Gallipoli.

We were now plunged into an intensive system of training such as we had never known. Though we did not realize it at the time, subsequent events proved clearly that every aspect of training as well as the operation itself had been carefully prepared by the army staff, closely supervised by Plumer, but under the direction of General Harington, his very able chief of the General Staff. Harington was a remarkable man by any standard who was later to be severely tested, and survive, in the glare of an international setting during the Chanak crisis. At this time he was known to comparatively few as a competent and friendly staff officer. His renown was soon to come as being responsible for the detailed training, preparation and execution of the limited but most successful Allied military operation of the war up to that time.

It was typical that during the training of our battalion Plumer himself inspected us at work, while Harington did so several times. This was characteristic of the way in which the Army Command missed nothing in detailed preparation for the battle, down to battalion and battery level, months before the event.

We had a taste of the thoroughness we might expect when we were allotted a training ground chosen to represent as closely as might be the terrain over which we had to advance and attack successive enemy lines. Over and over again we exercised across this ground to a meticulously accurate time-table. Flags represented the creeping barrage and over and over again we practised advancing in close time with it, until our rate of progress became almost automatic. This we did first by companies, then by battalions and finally as a brigade. In addition an elaborate small-scale model of the battle-field had been prepared and this novelty was keenly studied by every rifleman, who was encouraged to take his time and ask questions. Nothing was rushed. This applied particularly to the examination of areas behind the enemy line, most of which were concealed from us by the lie of the land.

Such elaborate preparation was not only valuable training but also a clever morale-building excercise, for it must be admitted that the moment we realized which sector this terrain and model represented, a chill dread descended upon us. It certainly did upon me, for we were to attack from the St Eloi craters, one of the most heavily mined areas of the whole front, where our lines were scarcely fifty yards away from the enemy and where every move of ours would be visible to him. How could we hope to assemble a battalion at night unseen and unheard in such conditions; and if the Germans saw or heard us, would they not blow their mine first or bring a barrage down on our close-packed companies. These and a score of other questions connected with the heavily defended succession of lines we were expected to capture daunted us.

I cannot remember when first we were told in detail what our objectives were, but I do recall an occasion when General Harington paid us a visit. This was probably in mid-April after our first spell of training, when our division moved into the St Eloi sector and into reserve behind it. Working parties were out day and night engaged in preparations for the attack, including the laying of cables. We were then in support near Ridge Wood and the general told us that he had come to find out whether we had any particular problems on our sector and, if so, whether there was anything the Army Command could do to help. Much encouraged by so human a concern from a general with his responsibilities, we spread our maps on the table in the battalion orderly room.

The colonel explained about the approach march, the difficulty of assembling the battalion unperceived so close to the enemy and the formidable problems presented by the lie of the land and the enemy's strongly fortified defences. While acknowledging this, Harington replied that against these odds we must set the very great power of our artillery preparation and support. He confirmed that on the day of the attack the barrage would be the responsibility of two divisional artilleries, our own and the First Division's. In addition there would be a powerful concentration of medium and heavy artillery and he gave us some impressive details of this. Finally there would be the mines, one of the largest of which was, as we knew, to be exploded on the left of our battalion sector. Our plans had been carefully laid and the enemy should be much shaken by the time we advanced behind our barrage.

While we were examining the maps of the enemy lines in detail, I said there was one point I would like to raise: our chief concern was not so much with the enemy's forward defences as with a middle distance objective, the Dammstrasse. This was a built-up drive which in peace time had apparently led to a neighbouring château. We believed that its embankment had been strongly fortified, probably concrete pill-boxes had been built into it, and it could give us and the battalion on our left any amount of trouble supposing we captured our first objective and deployed in the open to attack it.

Harington listened and nodded when I had done. The General Staff had, of course, given much thought already to the Dammstrasse and its bombardment, but there might be a case for giving it special attention. He would speak to the major general Royal Artillery and recommend that it should be made a particular target for destruction by 9·2s. He thought that we could safely count upon it that this would be done. It was, as the sequel will show.

This incident, important as it was to us, was also typical of the approach of Second Army staff to the whole operation, which certainly played a significant part in the victory which followed. 'Gentlemen, remember that the staff are the servants of the infantry' was Plumer's opening adjuration to officers appointed to serve on his headquarters on Cassel Hill, and if any subordinate forgot it he would not stay there long. This approach had had its influence as it seeped down to battery and company level, so that gradually we began to believe at least in the possibility of victory. Even so, we could not forget either our second battle on the Somme or the natural and man-made obstacles against us in the Ypres Salient. Thus it fell out that this was the only occasion in the war when I wrote a letter to my mother and to Marjorie on the eve of going into action. Afterwards, I was rather ashamed, for it was the least justified.

Most soldiers, even the least religious will pray sometime, in battle it was for many of us a prayer of fear. We each had, I suppose, one form of weakness. Some might try to strike a bargain. If, Almighty God, you will do this for me, I will promise reform, to obey the commandments scrupulously, or whatever the offer might be. For me the prayer was always at heart the same: Please God, if I am to be hit let me be slightly wounded or killed but not mutilated. I cannot explain what prompted this dread of the loss of limbs or other mutilation for life. To be killed did not seem all that bad. After Jack and Nicholas and so many young friends, perhaps it was that death in battle seemed, if not normal, at least acceptable. We may not have felt with Corneille:

> *Mourir pour le pays n'est pas un triste sort;*
> *C'est s'immortaliser par une belle mort*

but at least many had gone that way before, and it did not seem a business to make such a fuss about, especially if it was quick and with little suffering; but to be mutilated for life with all that this conjured up for me, I just had not the courage to face it.

*

In the second half of May we had another strenuous spell of training, 'for offensive operations' as our orders told us. This time the area was Eperleques and the weather kindly. The first week was once again company and battalion exercises, the second the brigade in attack. By now we could almost have gone through our movements with our eyes shut. The battalion's war diary, which it was my responsibility to keep, concludes soberly a week before the battle: 'The training was good and the health of the men was considerably improved by the change;' so were the memories of the Somme growing fainter.

Early in the morning of June 5th we began our moves into battle positions. A Company took over the front line at St Eloi 'between Middlesex Lane and Crater Lane' with B Company in close support. C and D took up positions in the Reserve G.H.Q. line, hard by our old friend of the winter, Ridge Wood. Meanwhile we established our battalion headquarters on the left of our front line in the mine shaft itself, where we were to remain for forty-eight hours. In this way we should be alongside the miners who were still actively engaged with their task. We would know each move in the mining and counter-mining on which everything depended and could also be well forward at the nearest point to the exploding mine when zero hour came. Our colonel thought this the right tactical position to provide for any last-minute change of plan owing to the failure of the mine to explode, or for any other cause.

Our miners belonged to a New Zealand sapper company, masters of their craft and a stalwart group of men who had crossed the world as volunteers for this perilous job. Friendly and more casual in approach to us and to each other than were we more inhibited Englishmen, they had no illusions about the risks they ran and would jest at times about the odds they faced in their suffocating subterranean world. Yet all this was in a calm, almost nonchalant vein. They were grand companions and soon brought us up to date on the state of play. The St Eloi area had been mined and counter-mined for the best part of two years. The surface was an interlocking spread of craters while down below the tunnelling continued from both sides.

About forty hours now remained until our mine was due to be blown. Meanwhile by crawling quietly forward a few paces with our guide and then lying deathly still, we began to hear the faint but unmistakable tap tap of the German sappers at work. The question was whether the enemy would allow our miners to go on with their work unimpeded for the forty hours they still needed. Our New Zealanders were sceptical about this and rightly so as it proved.

Crater fighting must have been one of the most unpleasant activities of the war and I was thankful to have had no first-hand experience of it. Apart from the constant danger of being blown up, our troops had orders in the event of a mine exploding, to seize and hold the further lip of the crater it made. As the Germans had presumably the same orders, the result was a bloody hand-to-hand affray within the compass of every new crater.

Our headquarters in the mine shaft served its purpose, despite my old enemy the rats which were even larger and bolder than their prototypes near the Brasserie. It was no easy job to keep our food out of their jaws. Our headquarters runners thought they had found a way. They strung up their rations by a cord from the roof of the dug-out and fell asleep.

By morning the rats had scrambled along the roof, down the rope and devoured the lot.

The forward lines of our sector presented another problem for me. The muddy condition of the ground had once again made it impossible to dig effective trenches. As a result sand-bag parapets replaced them, but such was the labour and danger of building, repairing and raising these parapets that they were usually low for the height of the average man, for my six feet they were lamentably so, with the result that inspecting our companies in their new positions as I had to do, was a crawling, scrambling, dirty and uncomfortable business. It was even worse for Colonel Jarvis who was my height and much broader and heavier as well.

Despite these minor vexations June 5th passed off quietly enough and by midnight I could report that all companies were in position with only small losses. This was better than anything we had achieved on the Somme, but still the over-looked character of the Salient dismayed us.

June 6th dawned a lovely summer's day and during it our guns, all now in place for the battle, showed what they could do. All day the bombardment lasted with artillery of every calibre. There was never a shell in reply, which surprised us. Our New Zealanders were convinced that something was brewing and we took what precautions we could.

*

Soon after dark, in the short summer night, the blow fell. The Germans laid down a heavy barrage on our mine shaft and its approaches. So intense was this, that we were sure it predicted a raid. Up went our rockets and down came our barrage on the German front line. As the lines were so close, the whole small area was soon a blazing inferno, through which no German raiding party emerged. Our barrage had seen to that, but theirs had cost us ten casualties. Young Mason, our intelligence officer, who had given me much help, and two riflemen, were killed and seven wounded. Sadly enough the colonel and I had been talking of Mason and his future only a few days before. The colonel had remarked that he should make a good adjutant one day and I had agreed. It is strange how in war when death is a near neighbour one projects plans without giving much thought to the part which enemy action may play, and yet is taken by surprise when it does.

The rest of the night was spent disposing the battalion for the attack. To avoid moving A and B Companies again, I leapfrogged C and D into the lead. By 2 a.m. we were in position, tight-packed in our limited space, then the Germans began to shell, not heavily, but enough to make me fear that they had spotted us. The repeat of a barrage such as they had put down a few hours earlier on our now crowded ranks would have been murderous. The battalion was tight-packed in this way as deliberate policy, because we wanted to get all companies forward so as to be clear of our front line within seconds of our zero hour, before the enemy's barrage came down upon it, as it had and would. We lay dead still for our lives, the shelling fell away and all was quiet until, just before our mines were due to explode, a spread of rockets and Very lights were fired from the German front line opposite to us; too late, for almost at once the men who had fired them were dead.

At ? 10 a.m. our mine exploded under the old mine craters and we leapt from our first line under cover of the barrage. The colonel and I were on the battalion's left flank with our headquarters, as near our mine as we dared be. It was an astonishing sight, rising like some giant mushroom to a considerable height in the air before it broke suddenly into fragments of earth, stones and timber falling over a wide area. The whole ground heaved so violently that for a fraction of a second we thought we were over the mine instead of beside it. As the barrage opened simultaneously, the noise of the guns deadened all sound from the mine, except that we could hear, even above this crescendo, the screams of the imprisoned Germans in the crater.

We could do nothing for them, for we had at all costs to keep up with our barrage. Our tactics were based on a close follow-up by the infantry to allow enemy machine-guns no pause to get into action before we were upon them. As it was, we captured a crew with what appeared to be a new type of machine-gun intact in one of the craters. Presumably they were too shaken by the mine explosion to do their job in time, but we had no illusion about the casualties that gun must have inflicted if it had got going. When the riflemen cleared the dug-outs which had not been blown in, they found watches hanging on nails which they avoided as possible booby traps, and hot tea and 'reindeer' sandwiches which they ate.

We found few enemy survivors among their forward positions, but it was at this early stage that I came upon the only fatal casualty I witnessed among our riflemen that day. The man had just fallen and lay spread-eagled on the ground, mortally wounded and already unconscious. I knew the rifleman for one of our most trusted soldiers and, for some reason I cannot explain, I was overwhelmed for a moment with most bitter sadness. Perhaps it was the helpless position in which his body lay, the sudden and pathetic waste of a young life, a boy determined to do his duty. It all seemed so miserably unfair. Quite possibly he had been hit by a fragment of our own barrage, but that altered nothing. He had done what he set out to do and by his firm will he had helped to save many lives, for which he had paid with his own. The momentary flash of that scene is still fresh in my mind.

For the rest of that day our attack succeeded beyond our wildest dreams. The Dammstrasse on our front had been virtually obliterated, as Harington had promised, and the Fusilier battalion on our left captured their stretch without loss. Even so, the dug-outs built into the bank and invisible from our side were immensely strong. Evidently we owed much to those 9·2s. As my official War Diary succinctly recorded in its final sentence on the day's fighting: 'The artillery bombardment and the barrage were excellent.'

So was the staff work. During the five hours which our advance was planned to last, we were scheduled to attack a series of lines, red, blue and black on our maps. The rate of our advance and the length of the pause at each captured objective was perfectly timed to give us just long enough to regroup before the barrage moved on again and the enemy no sufficient opportunity to rally and fight back.

Those five hours were, after the first roar, scramble and

confusion, a carefully ordered and executed advance, exactly as we had so repeatedly rehearsed. In the brilliant June sunshine I felt a rising sense of enthusiastic astonishment, of incredulity almost. This was so utterly unlike anything we had experienced before and so different from what we had expected. Despite all the practise attempts to convince us, we had not really believed at any time that we could capture all our objectives. If I had been asked before the battle what my inmost thoughts were, I should probably have said that we would be doing well if we captured the foremost organized trench system.

I saw no hand-to-hand fighting as the day wore on, though there was a momentary hold-up before a fortified and defended dug-out. This was on the site of an *estaminet* and on our immediate front, but our Lewis gunners did some skilful work on the flanks, out-manoeuvring the garrison. They fled and a few escaped into a neighbouring trench.

It was still only just after eight in the morning when we reached our final objective and saw dramatically spread before us on the ground the consequences of capturing the Messines ridge. On our immediate front the enemy was retiring his guns and infantry. This was a target such as we had never had in our sights before. Two companies of riflemen opened concentrated fire and the casualties the enemy suffered in the next half-hour were probably the heaviest of the day in this sector. I watched as the withdrawal became hurried and disordered under that raking rifle and Lewis-gun fire.

Our orders were to dig in when we had captured our final objective and prepare to meet a counter-attack. In the early evening we were to be relieved by a battalion of the Buffs from another division. No counter-attack developed. On the contrary we urged that our victorious gunners should be brought up to deal with the target now retreating beyond our range.

With the cynicism of a young man who thought himself old in battle, I remarked to the colonel that for sure we could not be relieved in such an advanced position that day; we would be lucky if our relief came at dawn. Once more I was proved wrong. The Buffs arrived on time to an eager welcome.

As we marched back in evening light over the ground we had captured and were nearing our old front line we saw our happiest sight of the war; our gunners had limbered up and were galloping forward over the old trenches on a hastily prepared way, up and on and over to take up their new positions and fire again upon the enemy we had just left. How we waved and shouted and cheered, for this had been their day.

When we got into camp that night, tired out as we were, we just had to discuss the events of the day. There were tales of a resounding victory and of thousands of prisoners. Our excitement was intense and we began to think that we were winning the war, that it might even soon be over. A pardonable illusion surely, but it was not to last long. Next morning I was able to make our own contribution to the general good news. Our casualties had been very slight; a total of seven killed and sixty-four wounded which included the ten casualties, three killed, of the night before the attack. We had no certain tally of the prisoners captured, but a first batch of eighty had been taken in the early fighting up to the Dammstrasse and about fifty more in the advance to our final objective. We felt proud and perhaps a little smug, but it was probably just as well that we had no idea of the long road still ahead.

*

Our respite proved shorter than we had expected. Within forty-eight hours the battalion was warned to get ready to return to the line, this time in the left sub-sector of our front, in Ravine Wood and near by the Ypres-Comines Canal. Here the attack had only been partially successful, progress limited and casualties heavier. It seemed that we were to take part in a minor sortie intended to improve our tactical position in preparation presumably for a wider attack. We took over our allotted sector on June 11th.

The next morning was my twentieth birthday and another day of glorious sunshine. When in the early hours I made a tour of our companies, the line seemed quiet enough and

Ravine Wood itself still leafy and summery with the birds singing. Our orders were to consolidate our existing line and build some new trenches and we set about our task as discreetly as we could, for we had no desire to alert the enemy. The battalion on our left had, if I remember right, the same kind of job to do.

The Germans were no doubt as conscious as we were that this sector was the only one where Plumer's Second Army had failed to take its objectives, and they were determined we should not get them now. As there was a lull on the whole of the rest of the army front, they could concentrate their artillery fire on this small area from which they concluded that an attack was soon to be launched.

They did just that and subjected us to the heaviest shell-fire any of us had ever known. Our casualties were many times higher than in the Messines battle the week before and added up to over two hundred in forty-eight hours from shell-fire alone, and it was machine-guns rather than shells that usually took the highest toll.

Our dappled wood was shattered, its trees broken and splintered across the ravine so that communication with and between the companies became slow and painful as well as dangerous. Only the weather never failed in long hours of unbroken sunshine. One morning I was trying with Iley to negotiate the congested broken trunks and branches in an attempt to reach D Company which had suffered at that time the heaviest losses. Our progress was exasperatingly slow and the shelling heavy so that we were scarcely half-way, though both young and very fit, when I had to pause for breath. Iley, usually the most imperturbable of men, heaved a sigh of relief, took off his tin hat despite the risk and wiping his face proclaimed 'Whew, sir, it's hot,' leaving it to me to determine whether he meant the sun or the shells. That was the nearest to a complaint I ever heard Iley utter, whether in my platoon or as my orderly when adjutant, in the two years we were together.

On June 14th we took part in a minor engagement which was reasonably successful. The battalion on our left attacked and captured a trench of some local importance while we established posts a few hundred yards in advance of our front line, as we had been ordered. The shelling continued unabated.

The next morning, soon after stand-down, the divisional commander visited us. As occasionally happened at that time of day there was a rare lull in the shelling. The general commented cheerfully upon this with some such remark as, 'This is much quieter than I was told it would be.' My C.O. was politely silent, but I had to comment sourly and not quite accurately, 'This is the only break in the shelling we have had since we have been here, sir.'

The truth is that we were all of us on edge by this time with shortage of sleep, the ceaseless bombardment and, saddest of all, the mounting casualties. We had worked hard in the last eight months to rebuild the battalion shattered by the Somme battles. We had been proud of the result and felt that the Messines battle had justified us. Now this wretched struggle of attrition was going to tear us apart again with nothing to show for it. I could not help seeing how haggard and spent our best officers and N.C.O.s looked and I was miserable. The red-eyed stage was back again.

Just before the Ravine Wood engagement began one of our senior officers had been appointed to a job at home. He was not a young man in years for an active command in the field, yet he had commanded a company and been badly wounded on the Somme and had returned to us to lead his company again at Messines. We were glad he was to have the rest he had so well earned, but he insisted that he must come up the line once more to say good-bye to us. This he did, leaving his horse a mile or so in the rear. Once mounted he would never see the war again. Our farewells exchanged he turned to go, when his eye fell on a package of letters, his company's mail waiting to go down the line. 'Can I take those with me for the last time?' he asked. 'Of course,' the colonel replied with a smile. Our guest stooped to pick up the small bundle and at that moment a shell burst beside him. He was gravely wounded. We managed to get him down the line, but he died at La Clytte and was buried there with some of his own riflemen.

Our battalion headquarters during these hideous days were in a strong concrete pill-box which had previously been either a German headquarters or possibly an advanced medical aid post. It was so well sited and stoutly built that the several days of bombardment before the Messines attack had not effectively damaged it. The interior was divided into a larger area, about three-quarters of the length, where the faithful signallers and orderlies were established, and a smaller cell beyond for the C.O., myself and our immediate staff. Outside, and for the full length of the building, ran a covered colonnade open to the east. As the enemy knew the exact location of this pill-box and shelled it constantly, we understood only too well how vulnerable that narrow corridor was to any chance or well-aimed shell. We had taken what precautions we could, including a warning notice not to loiter in the entrance.

At length on the sixth day came the orders and arrangements for relief, which was to take place at dusk. All went reasonably well for the greater part of this exercise. The shelling of our sector was intermittently heavy, but no more so than usual, and it did not appear that the relief had been spotted. One by one the messages came in from the companies that relief was complete and, with the last message, Jarvis and I were on our feet to leave when there was a resounding explosion which shook and swayed the pill-box and blew out all lights. A fraction of silence followed and then, all at once the clatter of falling masonry, timber, weapons and human bodies, groans from the wounded and dying, and over all an overwhelming stench of cordite, blinding and choking the survivors. I do not know how long it was before someone flashed a torch and we were able to see the damage we had already sensed as our brains cleared. A German 5·9 shell had come through the gap in the colonnade and burst in the doorway of our larger room when it was most crowded with the headquarters of the relieving battalion, which had now arrived, and our own people about to leave. Six weeks on the Somme and over a year of the varying fortunes of trench warfare had, we thought, inured us to any sights and smells, but this broke through to another layer of horror.

I cannot remember how long it took us to disentangle the dead from the dying, or how many hours we spent getting the wounded away to our first-aid post. Gradually the runners and signallers who had been out on duty came back and helped, but our eventual return to our support line was carried out in a daze.

What added personally to this numbing sense of shock was that several of the victims of this shambles had been working with me for two years, since we had joined up together. Almost all of them had been my daily companions and associates for the nine months since I had been appointed adjutant. I had grown to know them well and to respect them enormously. It is not enough to write that they had never failed in what they had been asked to do; they had so often done more than I could have expected of them. We had become so much a pattern, dovetailed into each other's work, that the survivors felt deeply sad and bereft as if they had lost a limb. War promoted working together into something good and true and rare, the like of which was never to be met with in civil life. It was our compensation, but this time it was not enough.

Two days in support and two more in reserve trenches and the battalion was back in the front line again, this time a little to the right of our previous sector. Though the German bombardment was still above average heavy, we had only to concentrate on strengthening our own line and our casualties were lighter, not least because our tour of duty was brief, only forty hours. On June 26th we were back in the Dammstrasse which had given us so much concern a few weeks earlier. One afternoon we heard the sound of several aircraft flying from east to west. As they swooped in pursuit of one of our machines, the sun struck the aircraft and we saw their red bellies. They were the Richthoften Squadron, but this time, to our relief, their intended victim got away.

Soon afterwards we were withdrawn further for a spell of rest, and leave for some. Among those who had earned and enjoyed it were the surviving riflemen from our headquarters.

. . .

It must have been in the latter half of May that I first learnt that I might be offered a junior post under Harington at Second Army headquarters. When Jarvis spoke to me about it, I had a definite view. In no circumstances could I leave the battalion until after the Messines engagement for which we had been training. Probably Jarvis expected this reply, which could hardly have been otherwise; but he urged me not to turn down the offer, only to ask that the opportunity should, if possible, be postponed. He pointed out that it would not be long before I had served a year as adjutant, added to this, I was now the only combatant officer to have served continuously with the battalion since it landed in France. He went on to say that if I were not a casualty I could hardly be adjutant for ever and, in the natural course of things, I could reasonably expect to be a brigade major. A spell at Second Army headquarters, where the standards were admittedly high, would be just the introduction for me if I could make the grade. We agreed to discuss these matters again after the battle and I made up my mind to do what I was told, if I survived.

Accordingly I became a G.S.O.3 at Second Army headquarters in July 1917 until, in the autumn, Plumer was sent to take command of our troops in Italy and Harington went with him. It was then I learned that Harington had recommended me to be a brigade major. After a further spell of duty as G.S.O.3 of a London Territorial Division, under General Cator's command, I found myself in the early spring of 1918 appointed brigade major with the 198th Infantry Brigade.

To be a brigade major was a job I had always coveted, whether seen from below as an adjutant or from the, to me, less congenial remoteness of divisional headquarters. The brigade and its staff seemed of exactly the right size and scope for individual efforts to be rewarding, while the contacts with units were close enough to have a human interest. This applied particularly to the last months of the war when the brigade could be expanded to include cavalry and artillery. The work was strenuous and, even by the standards of trench warfare, there was little chance of sleep; by day attack, by night preparing and issuing orders for the next advance. Mercifully the casualties were light.

Fortunately for me my brigadier, Alan Hunter, was an officer in my own regiment who had been through staff college and served as brigade major in the opening weeks of the war. He tolerated my shortcomings and the brigade was active in attacks against the enemy in the closing months of the war until Armistice Day. These events could not, however, have for me the same close personal character of comradeship as life with the Yeoman Rifles, where we had enlisted together, trained together, fought together. The more beastly and dangerous the conditions, the more this association seemed to count, which is perhaps why these memories mean so much to the survivors until this day.

It may be that as the years of war were also for some of us the years when we were very young, we have been apt to confuse the two and even to feel a sigh of regret when thinking of that time. The truth is that grief, and the sadness of parting, and sorrows that seem eternal are mitigated by time, but they leave their memories and their scars and we would not have it otherwise.

And so my war ended one June day in 1919 in a demobilization camp on the raw Wiltshire downs. I had entered the holocaust still childish and I emerged tempered by my experience and bereft of many friends, but with my illusions intact, neither shattered nor cynical, to face a changed world.

Index

In this volume of autobiography, Anthony Eden recalls the first twenty years of his life. He has described his political career in the three volumes of *The Eden Memoirs*. By contrast, this account of his childhood, his family background, and his experiences at an early age in the First World War, is highly personal. And in view of his later emergence as a world statesman, it is of special interest.

It is a narrative full of illuminating anecdote, of memorable and often eccentric characters, and one which, as social history, gives a remarkable picture of a life which was to vanish utterly in the horror of the First World War.

In the later part of the book, Anthony Eden gives a detailed, personal and often deeply moving account of his part in that war: in Flanders at the age of eighteen, an Adjutant at nineteen, and a Brigade Major at twenty; in the front line during the battles of the Somme and Messines; there was almost no aspect of the fighting he did not personally endure.

'My war ended,' he writes, 'one June day in 1919 in a demobilization camp on the raw Wiltshire downs. I had entered the holocaust still childish and I emerged tempered by my experience and bereft of many friends, but with my illusions intact, neither shattered nor cynical, to face a changed world.'